The Nation Must Awake

My Witness to the Tulsa Race Massacre of 1921

Mary E. Jones Parrish

FOREWORD BY
John Hope Franklin

INTRODUCTION BY
John Hope Franklin and Scott Ellsworth

AFTERWORD BY
Anneliese M. Bruner

TRINITY UNIVERSITY PRESS
SAN ANTONIO, TEXAS

Published by Trinity University Press
San Antonio, Texas 78212

Events of the Tulsa Disaster, by Mary E. Jones Parrish, was originally printed in 1923.

Afterword copyright © 2021 by Anneliese M. Bruner

Foreword, by John Hope Franklin, excerpted from Franklin's foreword to Scott
Ellsworth's *Death in a Promised Land: The Tulsa Race Riot of 1921* and the testimony
Franklin gave before a congressional committee considering the Tulsa-Greenwood Race
Riot Claims Accountability Act of 2007

Introduction, by John Hope Franklin and Scott Ellsworth, adapted from "History Knows
No Fences: An Overview," by John Hope Franklin and Scott Ellsworth, in *A Report by the
Oklahoma Commission to Study the Tulsa Race Riot of 1921*. Reprinted courtesy of the Estate
of John Hope Franklin and Scott Ellsworth

Cover illustration: *Black Blood, No. 3: In the Spirit of Mary Elizabeth Jones Parrish, Published
Author*, by Ajamu Kojo. Copyright © 2017 by Ajamu Kojo. Reprinted courtesy of the
artist

Author photo by Erin Schaff

Book design by BookMatters, Berkeley
Cover design by Anne Richmond Boston

ISBN 978-1-59534-943-9 paperback
ISBN 978-1-59534-944-6 ebook

Trinity University Press strives to produce its books using methods and materials in an
environmentally sensitive manner. We favor working with manufacturers that practice
sustainable management of all natural resources, produce paper using recycled stock, and
manage forests with the best possible practices for people, biodiversity, and sustainability.
The press is a member of the Green Press Initiative, a nonprofit program dedicated to
supporting publishers in their efforts to reduce their impacts on endangered forests,
climate change, and forest-dependent communities.

CIP data on file at the Library of Congress

25 24 23 22 21 | 5 4 3

The Nation Must Awake is a compilation. The core document, *Events of the Tulsa Disaster*, is an important historical record of one of the most significant—and most ignored—episodes in American history. Its author, Mary E. Jones Parrish, produced this remarkable collection of eyewitness accounts of the Tulsa race massacre of 1921, and we should be indebted to her. What the witness shared, alongside others in her community, is concise and impactful.

Since Parrish's work is a historical document, we have left her text intact, including language and phrasing that was common in her time though rightfully troublesome today. We know readers are able to understand that context and can assess the document, as well as the contemporary reflections provided by historians and Parrish's great-granddaughter. As a nonprofit publisher committed to close reexaminations of our lives, we thank readers for rediscovering this important book along with us.

TRINITY UNIVERSITY PRESS

Look up, lift up, and lend a helping hand [for] we cannot rise higher than our weakest brother.

Tonight as I write and think of Tulsa . . . my eyes well with tears and my soul cries for justice. Oh, America! Thou Land of the Free and Home of the Brave! The country that gave its choicest blood and bravest hearts to make the world safe for democracy! How long will you let mob violence reign supreme? Is democracy a mockery?

— MARY E. JONES PARRISH

» CONTENTS «

Smoke billowing over Greenwood after the riot, 1921.
Courtesy of the Library of Congress.

John Hope Franklin

In the spring of 1921 I was only six years old, but the events in Tulsa in late May and early June were permanently etched in my mind. For some years my family had been living in Rentiesville, an all-Negro village some sixty-five miles south of Tulsa. I was born there, in the post office, where my father was postmaster, the justice of the peace, president of the Rentiesville Trading Company, and the town's only lawyer. There was not a decent living in all those activities; and when my father left in February 1921, to open a law office in Tulsa, the family was to follow in the summer. As my mother completed her teaching stint in Rentiesville that spring, I was as anxious as my brother and sister (our older sister was away in a Tennessee boarding school) to move to the big city.

Then it happened! Tulsa was burning! The news of the Tulsa riot reached the little village slowly and piecemeal. In 1921 there were no radios or television sets, of course. And Rentiesville had no telephones, or even a telegraph to connect it with the outside world. We had to depend on news of the riot that was relayed from Tulsa to Muskogee, where it was printed in the *Daily Phoenix*, which was dropped off at

Rentiesville by the Katy Railroad mail and passenger train. Black Tulsa had been destroyed, burned out, we learned. Many blacks had been killed. But the paper did not say who they were, and we had no word from my father. Our mother put the best interpretation on the news, trying to allay our fears. It seemed like years before we learned a few days later that my father was safe.

In 1921 and for the next few years, the significance of the Tulsa riot to me was that it kept our family separated. The assets that my father had accumulated in those few months in Tulsa were destroyed in the riot, and our move there had to be postponed indefinitely. Meanwhile, my father was busy fighting city ordinances that seemed designed to obstruct black Tulsa's efforts to rebuild. In that, he was successful, but success in bringing the family together again came more slowly. His clients were poor people, and it took time to collect the small fees they could afford. Finally, on Thursday, December 10, 1925, my mother, who had quit her teaching job, packed our belongings and moved to the home in Tulsa that my father had rented for us.

Everyone who experienced the race riot in Tulsa or was touched by it in some way, as I was, had his own view of what happened, what was the aftermath, and what were the long-range consequences. When I arrived in Tulsa, at ten years of age, the collective wisdom in the black community had made certain conclusions about the riot. One was that Dick Rowland, whose allegedly improper advances toward a white girl precipitated the riot and who was later acquitted, was, along with all the black Tulsans, the victim of "riot fever" raging in the white community. Another was that many more whites were killed during the riot than any whites were willing to admit. If one went to court regularly, as I did with my father in the late twenties, one would be interested to hear cases involving the estate of some white person who died on or about June 1, 1921. One was always tempted to conclude that the deceased lost his life in the riot. Another view was that whites looted the homes of Negroes before burning them. Rumor had it that following the riot, Negro women would encounter white women wearing clothing or carrying some item recognized by the Negro women, who would simply claim the property and take it.

These conclusions seemed necessary for the continued self-esteem of Tulsa's black community. Whether or not the conclusions were valid, they had the desired effect. The self-confidence of Tulsa's Negroes soared, their businesses prospered, their institutions flourished, and they simply had no fear of whites. After 1921, an altercation in Tulsa between a white person and a black person was not a racial incident, even if there was a loss of life. It was just an incident. Such an attitude had a great deal to do with eradicating the fear that a Negro boy growing up in Tulsa might have felt in the years following the riot.

I believe in the long-term, the riot has cast a pall over the city, and has made it feel half-dead even today, decades later. Prior to the riot, the black community in Tulsa had been economically prosperous, not to mention spiritually and physically cohesive and strong. The riot was economically devastating, and given the lack of assistance and almost absolute segregation that existed for decades after the riot, people were not able to recover economically. The combination of circumstances that existed after the riot made it impossible for blacks in Tulsa to live as upstanding and fearless citizens even if they initially tried to do so. People did not just lose their homes and businesses, they seemed eventually to lose part of their dreams and their will, at least as a group. Thus, while I believe there was a period of approximately ten years in which people made their best effort to rebuild, and revitalize their community educationally and socially, eventually, given the economic devastation, and the persistent and complete separation and indifference of the white community, a pall of discouragement set in among the black community. And because the city has never honestly confronted what happened, that pall persists to this day.

John Hope Franklin and Scott Ellsworth

For those hearing about the 1921 Tulsa race riot for the first time, the event seems almost impossible to believe. During the course of eighteen terrible hours, more than one thousand homes were burned to the ground. Practically overnight, entire neighborhoods where families had raised their children, visited with their neighbors, and hung their wash out on the line to dry had been suddenly reduced to ashes. And as the homes burned, so did their contents, including furniture and family Bibles, rag dolls and hand-me-down quilts, cribs and photograph albums. In less than twenty-four hours, nearly all of Tulsa's African American residential district—some forty-square-blocks in all—had been laid to waste, leaving nearly nine thousand people homeless.

Gone, too, was the city's African American commercial district, a thriving area located along Greenwood Avenue that boasted some of the finest black-owned businesses in the entire Southwest. The Stradford Hotel, a modern fifty-four room brick establishment that housed a drugstore, barbershop, restaurant, and banquet hall, had been burned to the ground. So had the Gurley Hotel, the Red Wing Hotel, and the Midway Hotel. Literally dozens of family-run businesses—from cafes and mom-and-pop grocery stores to the Dreamland Theatre, the Y.M.C.A. Cleaners, the East End Feed Store, and Osborne Monroe's roller-skating rink—had also gone up in flames, taking with them the livelihoods, and in many cases the life savings, of literally hundreds of people.

The offices of two newspapers—the *Tulsa Star* and the *Oklahoma Sun*—had also been destroyed, as were the offices of more than a dozen doctors, dentists, lawyers, realtors, and other professionals. A U.S. Post Office substation was burned, as was the all-black Frissell Memorial Hospital. The brand new Booker T. Washington High School building escaped the torches of rioters, but Dunbar Elementary School did not. Neither did more than half a dozen African American churches, including the newly constructed Mount Zion Baptist Church, an impressive brick tabernacle that had been dedicated only seven weeks earlier.

Harsher still was the human loss. While we will probably never know the exact number of people who lost their lives during the Tulsa race riot, even the most conservative estimates are appalling. While we know that the so-called official estimate of nine whites and twenty-six blacks is too low, it is also true that some of the higher estimates are equally dubious. All told, considerable evidence exists to suggest that at least seventy-five to one hundred people, both black and white, were killed during the riot. It should be added, however, that at least one credible source from the period— Maurice Willows, who directed the relief operations of the

American Red Cross in Tulsa following the riot—indicated in his official report that the total number of riot fatalities may have run as high as three hundred.

We also know a little, at least, about who some of the victims were. Reuben Everett, who was black, was a laborer who lived with his wife Jane in a home along Archer Street. Killed by a gunshot wound on the morning of June 1, 1921, he is buried in Oaklawn Cemetery. George Walter Daggs, who was white, may have died as much as twelve hours earlier. The manager of the Tulsa office of the Pierce Oil Company, he was shot in the back of the head as he fled from the initial gunplay of the riot that broke out in front of the Tulsa County Courthouse on the evening of May 31. Dr. A. C. Jackson, a renowned African American physician, was fatally wounded in his front yard after he had surrendered to a group of whites. Shot in the stomach, he later died at the National Guard Armory. But for every riot victim's story that we know, there are others—like the "unidentified Negroes" whose burials are recorded in the now yellowed pages of old funeral home ledgers—whose names and life stories are, at least for now, still lost.

By any standard, the Tulsa race riot of 1921 is one of the greatest tragedies of Oklahoma history. Walter White, one of the nation's foremost experts on racial violence, who visited Tulsa during the week after the riot, was shocked by what had taken place. "I am able to state," he said, "that the Tulsa riot, in sheer brutality and willful destruction of life and property, stands without parallel in America."

Indeed, for a number of observers through the years, the term "riot" itself seems somehow inadequate to describe the violence and conflagration that took place. For some, what occurred in Tulsa on May 31 and June 1, 1921, was a massacre, a pogrom, or, to use a more modern term, an ethnic cleansing. For others, it was nothing short of a race war. But whatever term is used, one thing is certain: when it was all over, Tulsa's African American district had been turned into a scorched wasteland of vacant lots, crumbling storefronts, burned churches, and blackened, leafless trees.

Anyone who lived through the riot could never forget what had taken place. And in Tulsa's African American neighborhoods, the physical, psychological, and spiritual damage caused by the riot remained highly apparent for years. Indeed, even today there are places in the city where the scars of the riot can still be observed. In North Tulsa, the riot was never forgotten—because it could not be.

But in other sections of the city, and elsewhere throughout the state, the riot slipped further and further from view. As the years passed and, particularly after World War II, as more and more families moved to Oklahoma from out of state, more and more of the state's citizens had simply never heard of the riot. Indeed, the riot was discussed so little, and for so long, even in Tulsa, that in 1996 Tulsa County district attorney Bill LaFortune could tell a reporter, "I was born and raised here, and I had never heard of the riot."

How could this have happened? How could a disaster

the size and scope of the Tulsa race riot become, somehow, forgotten?

Nowhere was this historical amnesia more startling than in Tulsa itself, especially in the city's white neighborhoods. "For a while," noted former oilman Osborn Campbell, "picture postcards of the victims in awful poses were sold on the streets." More than one white ex-rioter "boasted about how many notches he had on his gun." But in time, the riot, which some whites saw as a source of local pride, came to be regarded more generally as a local embarrassment. Eventually, Osborn added, "the talk stopped."

So, too, apparently did the news stories. For while it is highly questionable whether—as has been alleged—any Tulsa newspaper actually discouraged its reporters from writing about the riot for years on end, the riot does not appear to have been mentioned in the local press.

Despite such official negligence, however, there were always Tulsans through the years who helped make it certain that the riot was not forgotten. Both black and white, sometimes working alone but more often working together, they collected evidence, preserved photographs, interviewed eyewitnesses, wrote about their findings, and tried, as best as they could, to ensure that the riot was not erased from history.

None, perhaps, succeeded as spectacularly as Mary E. Parrish, a young African American teacher and journalist. Parrish had moved to Tulsa from Rochester, New York, in

1919 or 1920, and had found work teaching typing and short-hand at the all-black Hunton Branch of the Y.M.C.A. With her young daughter, Florence Mary, she lived at the Woods Building in the heart of the African American business district. When the riot broke out, both mother and daughter were forced to abandon their apartment and flee for their lives, running north along Greenwood Avenue amid a hail of bullets.

Immediately following the riot, Parrish was hired by the Inter-Racial Commission to "do some reporting" on what had happened. Throwing herself into her work with her characteristic verve—and, one imagines, a borrowed type-writer—Parrish interviewed several eyewitnesses and tran-scribed the testimonials of survivors. She also wrote an ac-count of her own harrowing experiences during the riot and, together with photographs of the devastation and a partial roster of property losses in the African American commu-nity, published all of the above in the book *Events of the Tulsa Disaster*. While only a handful of copies appear to have been printed, Parrish's volume was not only the first book pub-lished about the riot—and a pioneering work of journalism by an African American woman—it remains, to this day, an invaluable contemporary account.

The destruction of Tulsa's Greenwood District, June 1, 1921.

EVENTS OF THE TULSA DISASTER

Mary E. Jones Parrish

AS PUBLISHED IN 1923

After the riot, June 1, 1921.
Courtesy of the Library of Congress.

I came from Rochester, N.Y., in 1918, to visit a brother who lived in Tulsa. In Rochester, our people were of a limited number, and the sole business engaged in was restaurants, hotels, rooming houses, barber shops, beauty parlors, etc. During my few months stay in Tulsa, my eyes feasted on the progressive sights they beheld among our group.

Every face seemed to wear a happy smile. This peace and happiness was destined to change to a deep and quiet sorrow, for it was at this time that the hand of the World War was felt most keenly here. Our Uncle Sam summoned 250 Black boys at one time. These boys did not hesitate, but bravely heeded the call, many never to return to their then beloved Tulsa. These brave boys gave their lives to make the world safe for democracy. Is it safe? Let Tulsa, the city that suffered thousands of its innocent, law-abiding citizens to be made homeless, answer.

We pray that God will be merciful and never let these noble Sons of Ham, whose life blood stains the soil of "No Man's Land," know what their loved ones and friends, whom they left behind, have been made to suffer.

Tonight as I write and think of Tulsa then and the Tulsa of June 1st, my eyes well with tears and my soul cries for justice. Oh, America! Thou Land of the Free and Home of the Brave! The country that gave its choicest blood and bravest hearts to make the world safe for democracy! How long will you let mob violence reign supreme? Is democracy a mockery? Is this beautiful "Land where our fathers died, the land of the Pilgrims' pride" to drift into Bolshevism and anarchism as Russia has done? If King Mob continues to rule it is only a matter of time until we shall witness some of the scenes of Russia enacted right here on our shores.

The rich man of power and the fat politician who have maneuvered to get into office, and even our Congress, may sit idly by with folded hands and say, "What can we do?" Let me warn you that the time is fast approaching when you will want to do something and it will be too late.

When mob violence first began, it originated in the South, and its victims were Black men and women. Today the hand of King Mob is being felt in all parts of the United States, and he is no respecter of persons, race or color—not even sparing white women.

The Dyer Anti-Lynch Bill's passage will be a glorious victory towards making the United States safe for its peaceful, law-abiding Black citizens. We, as a race, especially, doff our hats to Mr. Dyer, the originator of this bill, and to the noble men of Congress who voted for it. I cannot go further without paying respects to the sheriff of Kentucky, who so courageously defended his post of duty and the life of the prisoner placed under his care. Had America more men who, like him, respected their path of office, even to the extent of using a machine gun if necessary, we would have less lynching parties and racial troubles. The Tulsa Disaster was really caused by a threatened "Lynching Bee," and because the men of Color rose up in defense of the law and to protect a fellow man from the hands of the lawless horde that had gathered around the jail. (See extracts from the *Literary Digest* of June 18th.)

Just as this horde of evil men swept down on the Colored section of Tulsa, reducing the accumulation of years of toil and sacrifice to piles of brick, ashes and twisted iron, if something is not done to bring about justice and to punish them, thereby checking that spirit, just so will they, some future day, sweep down on the homes and business places of their own race. This spirit of destruction, like that of mob violence when it is once kindled, has no measure or bounds, neither has it any respect of place, person or color. At one time lynching was considered a Southern pastime. Today the land of the North has also been branded with this abominable sin and disgrace.

How recent seem the beginnings of this little book! It is my sincere hope and desire that it will serve the purpose of "Uncle Tom's Cabin," that is, that it will serve to open the eyes of the thinking people of America to the impending danger of letting such conditions exist and remain within the "Land of the Free and Home of the Brave," and to pay a tribute to the martyrs of the Tulsa Disaster and massacre.

This was the idea of the story, and with this little prefatory word I commend it to those who may chance to read it.

After the riot, showing Mount Zion Baptist Church.
Courtesy of the Library of Congress.

My Experience in Tulsa

After visiting Tulsa in 1918, I returned to Rochester, and remained there only five months before being called to McAlester, to the bedside of my dear mother who departed this life after six months of patience and care by the children who loved her so dearly. I then decided to locate in Tulsa. I had heard of this town since girlhood and of the many opportunities here to make money. But I came not to Tulsa as many came, lured by the dream of making money and bettering myself in the financial world, but because of the wonderful co-operation I observed among our people, and especially the harmony of spirit and action that existed between the business men and women.

On leaving the Frisco station, going north to Archer Street one could see nothing but Negro business places. Going east on Archer Street for two or more blocks there you would behold Greenwood Avenue, the Negro's Wall Street, and an eyesore to some evil-minded real estate men who saw the advantage of making this street into a commercial district. This section of Tulsa was a city within a city, and some malicious newspapers take pride in referring to it as "Little Africa."

On Greenwood one could find a variety of business places which would be a credit to any section of the town. In the residential section there were homes of beauty and splendor which would please the most critical eye. The schools and many churches were well attended.

Space will not permit me to give a full description of the Tulsa folk here. "Tulsa, Then and Now," by Prof. G. A. Gregg, A.B., which follows will give a mental view of our group in Tulsa.

After spending years of struggle and sacrifice, the people had begun to look upon Tulsa as the Negro Metropolis of the Southwest. Then the devastating Tulsa Disaster burst upon us, blowing to atoms ideas and ideals no less than mere material evidence of our civilization.

A Colored boy accidentally stepped on a white elevator girl's foot. An evening paper hurled the news broadcast, with the usual "Lynching is feared if the victim is caught." Then the flames of hatred which had been brewing for years broke loose.

Since the lynching of a White boy in Tulsa, the confidence in the ability of the city official to protect its prisoner had decreased; therefore, some of our group banded together to add to the protection of the life that was threatened to be taken without a chance to prove his innocence. I say innocence because he was brought to trial and given his liberty; the girl over whom the trouble was caused failed to appear against him.

On the evening of May 31st, I was busy with a class in

Typewriting until about 9 P.M. After my pupils were gone I immediately began reading a book which I was very anxious to finish (must admit, however, that I was never able to complete it), so did not notice the excitement until a late hour. The evening being a pleasant one, my little girl had not retired, but was watching the people from the window. Occasionally she would call to me, "Mother, look at the cars full of people." I would reply, "Baby, do not disturb me, I want to read." Finally she said, "Mother, I see men with guns." Then I ran to the window and looked out. There I saw many people gathered in little squads talking excitedly. Going down stairs to the street I was told of the threatened lynching and that some of our group were going to give added protection to the boy.

I am told that this little bunch of brave and loyal Black men who were willing to give their lives, if necessary, for the sake of a fellow man, marched up to the jail where there were already over 500 white men gathered, and that this number was soon swelled to over a thousand. Someone fired a stray shot and, to use the expression of General Grant, "All hell broke loose." From that moment quiet and peaceful Tulsa was turned into a hot-bed of destruction.

My little girl and I watched the excited groups from our window until a late hour, when I had her lie down and try to rest while I waited and watched. Waited and watched, for what—I do not know. One could hear firing in quick succession and it was hours before the horror of it all dawned upon me. I had read of the Chicago Riot and of the Washington trouble, but it did not seem possible that prosperous Tulsa, the city which was so peaceful and quiet that morning, could be in the thrall of a great disaster. When it dawned upon me what was really happening I took my little girl in my arms, read one or two chapters of Psalms of David and prayed that God would give me courage to stand through it all.

The Frisco tracks and station form a dividing line between the business section of White Tulsa and Black Tulsa. It was here that the first battle was staged. Like mad bulls after a red flag or blood thirsty wolves after a carcass, so did these human wolves called men rave to destroy their fellow citizens. But these brave boys of ours fought gamely and held back the enemy for hours. Owing to the shortage of ammunition they were forced to retreat from Cincinnati, and immediately the advancing force began to pillage and burn that section.

About 1:30 o'clock the firing had somewhat subsided and it was hoped that the crisis had passed over. Someone on the street cried out, "Look, they are burning Cincinnati!" On looking we beheld columns of smoke and fire and by this we knew that the enemy was surging quickly upon Greenwood. Like Stonewall Jackson of old our boys stood "Like a stone wall," offsetting each and every attempt to burn Greenwood and the immediate vicinity. I had no desire to flee but my heart went out in sympathy for those who were fighting so bravely against such tremendous odds. I forgot about personal safety and was seized with an uncontrollable desire to see the outcome of the fray. The firing and burning continued at long intervals. In the early morning, about 3 or 4 o'clock, the Midway Hotel was seen to be burning. A friend in the building with me called up the Fire Department. The answer was, "They will be out right away," but they failed to show up. About 5 o'clock a lady friend called up the Police Department and asked how soon the Militia would reach Tulsa, and the reply was, "About 7 o'clock." Looking south out of the window of what then was the Woods Building, we saw car loads of men with rifles unloading up near the granary, which is located on the railroad tracks near First Street. Then the truth dawned upon us that our men were fighting in vain to hold their dear Greenwood. A fit of restlessness seized us and Mrs. Jones and I walked the halls, looking first out of the windows and then out of the doors. In our excitement we would sometimes forget ourselves and lean out of the window, when we would receive a timely warning to get back or be shot. At an early hour the lights were all out, so we prayed for daylight in hope that the worst would be over, but not so, for daylight had a distressing surprise in store for us.

After watching the men unload on First Street where we could see them from our windows, we heard such a buzzing noise that on running to the door to get a better view of what was going on, the sights our eyes beheld made our poor hearts stand still for a moment. There was a great shadow in the sky and upon a second look we discerned that this cloud was caused by fast approaching aeroplanes. It then dawned upon us that the enemy had organized in the night and was invading our district the same as the Germans invaded France and Belgium. The firing of guns was renewed in quick succession.

People were seen to flee from their burning homes, some with babes in their arms and leading crying and excited children by the hand; others, old and feeble, all fleeing to safety. Yet, seemingly, I could not leave. I walked as one in a horrible dream. By this time my little girl was up and dressed, but I made her lie down on the dufold in order that the bullets must penetrate it before reaching her. By this time a machine gun had been installed in the granary and was raining bullets down on our section. Looking out of the back door I saw people still fleeing and the enemy fast approaching. I heard a man groan; I looked up just in time to see him fall, and was pulled into the house. Still I could not flee. Finally my friend called her husband, who was trying to take a little rest, and they decided to try to make for a place of safety, so called to me that they were leaving. By this time the enemy was close upon us, so they ran out of the south door, which led out on Archer Street, and went east toward Lansing. I took my little girl by the hand and fled out of the west door on Greenwood. I did not take time to get a hat for myself or baby, but started out north on Greenwood, running amidst showers of bullets from the machine gun located in the granary and from men who were quickly surrounding our district. Seeing that they were fighting at a disadvantage our men had taken shelter on the buildings and in other places out of sight of the enemy. When Florence Mary and I ran into the street it was vacant for a block or more. Someone called to me to "Get out of the street with that child or you both will be killed." I felt that it was suicide to remain in the building, for it would surely be destroyed and death in the street was preferred, for we expected to be shot down at any moment, so we placed our trust in God, our Heavenly Father, who seeth and knoweth all things, and ran on out Greenwood in the hope of reaching a friend's home who lived over the Standpipe Hill in the Greenwood Addition. As I neared the hill I could see homes on Eastern and Detroit burning, and also discovered that the enemy had located on the hill and that our district was entirely surrounded. We thought that we were leaving the firing behind, but found that our danger was increasing for a machine gun was located on the hillside. As we neared the addition we caught up with other people fleeing in the same direction. We finally reached my friend's home, but to our disappointment found that she and her family had fled after watching for me all though the night. I then decided to follow the crowd in the hope of reaching safety. On and on we went toward the section line, the crowd growing larger and larger. The question on every lip when a newcomer from town would arrive was, "How far had they burned when you left town?"

At the section line I met Mrs. Thompson, her husband and family. They were on a truck and had started east. She called to me and I ran to them and got on the truck. Soon we had started again on our quest for safety. On and on we went, past many farm houses, mostly White. They looked at us as if we were animals escaping a forest fire. We passed many of our group. The most pathetic sight was an old couple struggling along on foot. How I longed to get off and

give them my seat, but I dared not leave my little girl alone
to perish. When we passed, the old lady asked us to take her
coat; it was too heavy. We did but have never been able to
find her again. After we had gone several miles we began to
see automobile loads of men with guns going east ahead of
us. We wondered where they were going but we were not
destined to wonder long, for as we neared the aviation fields
we saw their destination. The planes were out of the sheds,
all in readiness for flying, and these men with high-powered
rifles were getting into them. As we went further we saw
several men leaving the fields, going to the house, returning
with guns and heading towards Tulsa.

After we had traveled many miles into the country and
were turning to find our way to Claremore, we looked up
the road and saw a race lady coming toward us. My lady
friend and I went to meet her. She advised us to not try to
pass through a little adjoining town, for they were treating
our people awfully mean as they passed through, taking their
guns from them and threatening to place them in prison.
She made us welcome to come to her home and remain
until it was safe to return to Tulsa. We gratefully accepted
her hospitality and returned with her to her home. There we
rested and were as comfortable as could be expected under
the circumstances. Having been out in the hot sun all day
without hats—only makeshifts made from leaves—we found
the shelter of a roof very refreshing,

A bread wagon met the fleeing people on the roadside
and sold the bread. On the way we bought bread so when we

stopped to rest we had bread and water, whenever and wherever we could get it. Ofttimes the men would stop and dip water from a branch, using their hats for cups. In France? No, in Oklahoma. After reaching this home the crowd thronged there was too large to supply them out of a pail so a washtub was drafted into service and pride cast to the wind. We were so famished and our lips parched, the children crying for a drink, that this was the best tasting water we could remember of having tasted. I can never forget a family who started out and had the misfortune to lose one wheel off of their wagon and, therefore, had to get out and walk. In that number was a mother and father with a six-months-old infant—such a fine and healthy baby. The father would run along and carry it awhile when the mother would take it until she was tired out. When they both were just about exhausted the father cried out, "Will someone help us?" Being a mother, naturally my heart was in deep sympathy for them, so I called to them to bring the baby to me and I would care for it awhile and let them rest. They finally succeeded in getting another wheel, after going miles on the hub of the broken wheel.

The aeroplanes continued to watch over the fleeing people like great birds of prey watching for a victim, but I have not heard of them doing any harm to the people out in the direction where we were. I have been reliably informed, however, that they fired on the people who were gathered in groups in the Colored park close to town.

Everything went well until late in the afternoon. An elderly man with some daughters and grand-children came to

where we were stopping. He was sent to a nearby farm store
to procure food for the family. There he was told that the
Red Cross workers were coming out in trucks to bring food
to the suffering people and to take back to town all who
desired to go. Instead of buying food, as he was instructed
to do by his daughters, he informed the store people that
there were "lots of people" up where he came from desiring
food. They told him that they would send the trucks right
up on their return from town, which they did, but when the
trucks came they found no one to take back. After spending such a dreadful night and day and witnessing so much
destruction, how could we trust a race that would bring it
about? At that hour we mistrusted every person having a
white face and blue eyes. Since, we have learned that the Red
Cross workers came like angels of mercy to heal and help
suffering humanity. When the man told us what he had done
the crowd started out to look for another haven of rest. We
walked about two miles across the prairie, most of the way
having to carry the children to keep the weeds from stinging
their tired little limbs. We were well paid for the walk for
these kindly people prepared hot lunch for the bunch and
provided us with a place to sleep, so we remained here for
the night. Altho we were over thirteen miles from Tulsa we
could, at about 10 P.M., see the smoke rising from the ruins.

The next morning we were up bright and early, alert, listening, to see what we could learn. About 10 o'clock a White
man came out in a car to get a man who worked for him. He
informed us that Greenwood had been burned. It was then

that I shed my first tears. We spent the remainder of the day and night here and the next morning resolved to return and view the ruins of devastated Tulsa. That morning while waiting for the Red Cross truck to come for us we saw a man who had become separated from his wife and believed her to be shot off a hill side. He said that they were firing on them as they ran, none of the shots taking effect. We learned later, however, that his wife had only ran down the hill side and in that way they had become separated.

The Red Cross truck arrived for us about 9 o'clock and we started for Tulsa immediately, reaching there at an early hour. We did not enter there through our section of town, but they brought us in through the White section, all sitting flat down on the truck looking like immigrants, only that we had no bundles. Dear reader, can you imagine the humiliation of coming in like that, with many doors thrown open watching you pass, some with pity and others with a smile? We were stopped at the Exposition Park. Here we saw hundreds of our group huddled in like so many cattle and guarded. In the department where the women had been corralled were many army cots. They were also issuing out clothing and sandwiches. Here again I breathed a prayer to the Heavenly Father for strength. There were to be seen people who formerly had owned beautiful homes and buildings, and people who had always worked and made a comfortable, honest living, all standing in a row waiting to be handed a change of clothing and feeling grateful to be able to get a sandwich and glass of water. Somehow, I was tempted to get

off and share my fate with the rest, but my friend's home was
not burned so, being asked by her to accompany them home,
I accepted the invitation. Leaving the Exposition Park we
rode for blocks through the White district where we proved
to be an interesting spectacle. Soon we reached the district
which was so beautiful and prosperous looking when we
left. This we found to be piles of bricks, ashes and twisted
iron, representing years of toil and savings. We were horror
stricken, but strangely we could not shed a tear. For blocks
we bowed our heads in silent grief and tried to blot out the
frightful scenes that were ahead of us. One thing we noticed
was that every one of our group that we met was wearing a
tag inscribed "POLICE PROTECTION." On asking the meaning of this we were told that the town was under Martial
Law and all of our group had to wear these badges in order
to be permitted to come out on the streets and that everyone
had to be indoors before seven o'clock. All of the places of
business were also closed by this time. At last we reached my
friend's home to find it still standing but with everything
torn up and a part of her things gone. After preparing lunch
and resting awhile, we retired for the night.

Arising early the next morning we were greeted by another bright and beautiful day, but, indeed, a sad one. Our
hearts felt burdened and heavy as one feels after returning
from the last rites over a loved one. Being alone in the midst
of all this distress, with only my little girl, I felt that I had
not a moment to lose, so I dressed hurriedly, ate a bite and
rushed up town to see what was going on. I felt as if I was

in a wilderness of darkness and did not know which way to go. However, in looking around I found that the High School building was still standing, so was making my way towards it when on observing more closely I saw a big white streamer with a red cross on it. Then I felt more relieved, for this meant that THE MOTHER OF THE WORLD was close at hand and was not forgetting any of her children in distress, even tho they had black faces. When I was close enough to read the sign I read, "HEADQUARTERS OF THE AMERICAN RED CROSS." I breathed a prayer of thanks. Across the street I saw a big white tent and on looking up I read "Y.M.C.A. HEADQUARTERS." I felt pangs of joy, for this meant to me that I was getting in close touch with friends again, having had charge of the class in typewriting and shorthand under the Y.M.C.A. up until the fateful night. I passed by for I was on my way to the telegraph office to try to get in touch with my people. I succeeded in reaching my brother Reuben in McAlester over long distance. He had heard that my little girl and I were burned in the building, as no one had seen us leave it. He also urged me to leave Tulsa immediately, but I wanted to see affairs through so decided to remain in stricken Tulsa.

Returning to the Red Cross Headquarters I found long rows of women, men and children waiting their turn to receive clothing such as was obtainable. And the thing that I could not understand was why these innocent people, who were as helpless as babes, were placed under guard. Nevertheless, heavily armed guards were all around the building. Some were kind and manly, others were beasts dressed in uniforms. These poor people stood for hours waiting their turn; some were seen to sicken and faint. The nurses would immediately take them out of line and give them treatment.

I finally succeeded in getting inside of the door where I was met by a guard who asked what I wanted. On being told I was directed to a room where I was registered. From here I went upstairs into the clothing room in quest of a change of clothing for my little girl. Here I found stacks of clothing and shoes. Having worked hard always for an independent living, thereby being able to have what I wanted within reason, this was wormwood and gall to me, just to be standing around waiting to get a change of secondhand clothing, but what could I do? What we had on were soiled, they being all we had, and I was not yet permitted to go to town and purchase more. I succeeded in getting a change. On leaving this room everyone was searched to see that no one had more than a change. (Horrors!) Down stairs in the office I found telegrams from loved ones and friends who were trying to locate me. I immediately answered them. Everyone said "Leave Tulsa at once." I answered, "Am safe but cannot leave now."

Leaving the Red Cross Headquarters I went over to the Y.M.C.A. tent. There were gathered many people shaking hands and greeting each other like soldiers following a great battle. All seemed anxious to relate his or her experience. This organization furnished cold water for many thirsty throats. It also had a relief department in one side and two women employed to distribute clothing. Here one felt free to come and spend hours meeting friends. Posted in conspicuous places over the grounds around these places were lists of letters and telegrams.

In order to help the people get in touch with their loved ones who were anxious to hear from them, Mr. Theo Baughman, of the *Oklahoma Sun*, succeeded in getting out a little daily paper, and each day he would publish these lists. Each day the people sat under the tent and watched for these lists as well as for the lists of dead in the big dailies.

On arriving home this afternoon I found Brother Edward, who had risked the danger of passing by armed guards (entrances to our district were heavily guarded and everyone was required to have a "Police protection" badge to enter) to come for me. He insisted that I return home with him. Again I resolved to stay in Tulsa and see the outcome of this calamity.

Days passed without any important change in matters. Everyone seemed nervous and undecided what to do. Brother Harrison had written me to come to him at Langston. I was preparing to go when I was engaged by Rev. H. T. S. Johnson, of the Inter-Racial Commission, to do some reporting for that organization.

This proved to be an interesting occupation, for it helped me to forget my trouble in sympathy for the people with whom I daily came in contact. Up to this time I had worn no badge. A lady friend and I had business up town one very rainy day, and on returning home we were approached by a guard who demanded to see our cards. On being told we had no cards we were accordingly ordered to return to the city hall and get them. This was a perplexity for us in that one had to have some white person vouch for them regardless of their station in life before the trouble. We went to the City Hall. There I met Prof. Gregg, Executive Secretary of the Y.M.C.A. We explained our plight to him; he in turn offered to assist us. He explained to an officer in charge that I had been engaged in Y.M.C.A. work, even showed him the check for three months' work which he had just paid me. This check was signed by the Executive Secretary of the Central Y.M.C.A., up town, yet it would not serve as a passport to secure a card. As I had never worked for any white person in Tulsa I was at a loss just what to do. It was plainly shown that a white man's word was the only requirement to receive a card. I pondered just what to do, then I thought of a business firm and called them up. They came down and identified me and that was sufficient. I received my card without any trouble.

THE EMERGENCY HOSPITAL

The primary rooms of the Booker Washington School were converted into an emergency hospital. I can never erase the sights of my first visit to the hospital. There were men wounded in every conceivable way, like soldiers after a big battle. Some with amputated limbs, burned faces, others minus an eye or with heads bandaged. There were women who were nervous wrecks, and some confinement cases. Was I in a hospital in France? No, in Tulsa. One mother was so thoughtless as to burden her infant for life with the name of "JUNE RIOT."

AS A REPORTER

During the weeks that I served as a reporter I interviewed many people and no two had the same experience to tell. I was informed that the dead were so quickly disposed of on that night and day that it was impossible to ever get an exact record of the dead and wounded. I was further informed that the enemy was well prepared, as a conquering army going out to battle, with ambulances and trucks to pick up and care for the dead and wounded.

One lady told me that she saw a woman shot, not mortally, just ahead of her while fleeing for safety; and another was seen to become a mother before she could reach a place of safety.

Everyone with whom I met was loud in praise of the State troops who so gallantly came to the rescue of stricken Tulsa. They used no partiality in quieting the disorder. It is the general belief that if they had reached the scene sooner many lives and valuable property would have been saved. Just as praise for the State troops was on every tongue so was denunciation of the Home Guards on every lip. Many stated that they fooled them out of their homes on a promise that if they would give up peacefully they would give them protection as well as see that their property was saved. They surrendered and were taken to the various places of safety, where they were cared for by that kindly angel of mercy, the Red Cross. When they returned to what were once their places of business or homes, hopes built upon the promises

of the Home Guards, how keen was their disappointment to
find all of their earthly possessions in ashes or stolen. (Read
testimonials.)

About this time a body of loyal race men called a meeting
at the First Baptist Church and organized THE COLORED
CITIZENS' RELIEF COMMITTEE and the EAST END WEL-
FARE BOARD. Before the smoke of the massacre had blown
over the City Dads had gotten their heads together and
succeeded in passing a new fire ordinance to prevent these
poor homeless people from rebuilding on their homes again.
These men worked faithfully and have fought many battles
for their fellow man. They looked after the needs of the people both physically and legally to the best of their ability,
with the assistance of the outside world. It was through the
inspiration supplied by this committee, working in harmony
with the Red Cross, that Greenwood has been rebuilt today.

LESSONS OF THE DISASTER

The Tulsa Disaster has taught great lessons to all of us, has
dissipated some of our false creeds, and has revealed to us
verities of which we were oblivious. The most significant
lesson it has taught me is that the love of race is the deepest
feeling rooted in our being and that no race can rise higher
than its lowest member.

Some of our group who have been blest with educational
or financial advantages are ofttimes inclined to forget ourselves to the extent that they feel their superiority over those
less fortunate, but when a supreme test like the Tulsa Disaster

comes, it serves to remind us that we are all of one race; that human fiends, like those who had full sway on June 1st, have no respect of person. Every Negro was accorded the same treatment, regardless of his education or other advantages. A Negro was a Negro on that day and was forced to march with his hands up for blocks. What does this teach? It should teach us to "Look Up, Lift Up and Lend a Helping Hand," and remember that we cannot rise higher than our weakest brother.

"Comfort the feebleminded; support the weak." I Thes. 5:14.

Testimonials of the Tulsa Riot

TULSA, OKLA., JUNE 20, 1921

The first information that I received of the Riot came about 9:30 o'clock Tuesday night, May 31st, 1921. I was attending a play given by the Senior Class. A little boy came up, almost out of breath, and exclaimed, "They are trying to lynch a Colored man down town and the Colored people are going down to prevent it."

The meeting broke up in some confusion and all went home. We sat up at our house till about midnight and then we decided to go to bed. There was little sleeping, for the noise of guns kept us awake all night.

About 5 o'clock a very peculiar whistle blew. This seemed to have been a signal for a concerted attack by the whites, for immediately a terrible gun fire began. Aeroplanes also began to fly over very low; what they were doing I cannot say for I was in my room.

About 5:30 someone called up our home and said for the men not to fight for the Home Guard were visiting the homes and searching them, but that they would harm no one. A few minutes after that some men appeared with drawn guns and ordered all men out of the house. I went out immediately. They ordered me to raise my hands, after which three or four men searched me. They told me to line up in the street. I requested them to let me get my hat and best shoes but they refused and abusively ordered me to line up. They refused to let one of the men put on any kind of shoes. After lining up some 30 or 40 of us men they ran us through the streets to Convention Hall, forcing us to keep our hands in the air all the while. While we were running some of the ruffians would shoot at our heels and swore at those who had difficulty in keeping up. They actually drove a car into the bunch and knocked down two or three men.

When we reached Convention Hall we were searched again. There people were herded in like cattle. The sick and wounded were dumped out in front of the building and remained without attention for hours.

James T. A. West
Teacher in a High School

>«

TULSA, OKLA., JUNE 21, 1921

Roomers came in and told me that the White people were burning the Colored people's homes on Archer Street. Then I heard guns firing; this continued until early in the morning, when everyone ran away and left two other men and me. Later the Guards came, told one of these men to come out, but he replied "I am shot"; he then fell in my house, shot through the back. Then I came out of the house and tried to save something but failed.

My greatest loss was my beautiful home and my family Bible. I am 92 years of age so they failed to bother me. I came up Easton to Frankfort Street, ran through the pipe yard, was nearly overcome by smoke but was rescued and carried to Convention Hall. Mrs. Johnson (White), of St. Louis, took me to the Catholic Church. I remained there until about 2 o'clock, then was carried to the Fair Grounds by the Red Cross, then brought back to the Methodist Church. A Colored lady told me to come to her house and live, but when we got there her home was in ashes. Mr. Williams (Colored), then took me in charge and I was afterwards taken over again by the Red Cross and kept out at the Park. Then I was recommended to some White man who would take care of me. There had been some Colored people to ask about me, one a very dear friend of mine. As I have no children or relation, I had planned to will her my valuable property even before this happened for she has treated me as a father. They did not let her take me, but as they have let me out to go to the White man, I think I shall go to her instead, as I would like for my property to fall to my own race. This is the worst scene that I have ever witnessed in my 92 years.

Jack Thomas

»«

TULSA, OKLA., JUNE 22, 1921

On the night of the Riot we had our class of Bible study, as usual. After the class was over, and far into the night, we heard shooting down town, which we could only interpret to mean that there was trouble of some kind. We went into the house and went to bed listening to the spasmodic shooting, which clearly convinced us that there was trouble.

In the morning the shooting was more severe in front of our house. The Whites were firing on Colored, who, seemingly unaware of the trouble, were on their way to work, and in passing were met with vollies of shot. We remained in the house until some folks came and stated that if we wanted protection we had better go to Convention Hall at once. This we promptly did, leaving our house partly open. About two o'clock we were called for by some White friends and brought back to our home to find everything considerably tumbled around, but no serious damage done.

We found a White gentleman in charge of the house, who related to us that himself and his son and a few neighboring White friends had prevented any further molestation of our home. They stated that they were ready to stay with us all night if we thought it necessary to ensure that we would not be molested.

My principal loss was a two-story brick building on Greenwood Street. (Of course, we lost some clothes, shoes, money and other things in the house that we did not consider worthwhile.)

As to preventing such mob violence, I refer you to my

statements in the *Oklahoma Sun*, Tulsa, Okla.; the *Black Dispatch*, Oklahoma City; the *Muskogee Cimeter*, Muskogee, Okla. That is the best solution I know of for race riots and mob violence.

Richard J. Hill, Atty
International Bible Student

»«

TULSA, OKLA., JUNE 22, 1921

On Tuesday evening, about 9:30 o'clock, I heard the report that they were going to mob a Colored boy, but my family and I remained at home. Then we heard firing. I ran for my daughter, then a man and his family came running by and he said, "The Whites have burned my home and over $7,000.00." His wife had on about one piece. Then a crowd came and reported that they were burning and killing as they went (meaning the Whites were killing and burning). I ran behind a cabinet but they were crowding us so closely that I ran out to an out house where I began to pray. Then the crowd of Whites ordered everybody to come out of the house, but they were slow about coming out so the ruffians shot against the house. I ran further and saw about fifteen White men chasing a man who was helpless—they even fired at him, but missed. I then went upon the hill carrying a small bundle of clothes and bedding.

I was lost from my daughter and her baby until late in the afternoon Wednesday. I saw about five women faint. At the Presbyterian Church I saw about four little children who were lost from their mothers. Old and young had to pile on trucks and when we were being driven through town men were seen clapping their hands rejoicing over our condition.

Mrs. Roseatter Moore

>‹‹

TULSA, OKLA., JUNE 22, 1921

Immediate Cause: There was a report in the *Tulsa Tribune* that threats were being made to lynch a Negro for attempted criminal assault upon a White girl, which was wholly without foundation or cause.

Second: White men reading this report gathered at the jail to take part in the lynching and the Negroes, seeing this gathering, rightly concluded that lynching was the object of the White people, and consequently armed themselves and came on the scene and offered their support and assistance to the sheriff. While this was in progress a fight between some Whites and Negroes was started which resulted in several members of each side being shot. The Negroes then left the Court House and came to the East End, leaving a guard at every approach to the Negro quarter.

Desultory firing on both sides was kept up for several hours, when the Negroes, believing all danger of an invasion by the Whites over, went to their homes. But, during this time and unknown to them, plans for an armed invasion of the Negro quarter by the Whites under protection of the city and county police had been under way. The avowed purpose of this invasion was to disarm the Negroes and to corral the men or arrest them that they might not do any further harm. They (the Whites) did this and in most cases met with no resistance except in cases where no reason was given by the Whites for entering the Negro homes, and this was generally the rule. The Negro did not know whether he was being called out to be shot, or what, for shooting was all he could hear or see. If he submitted without question he was taken to jail, but if he dared to question the intruder he was shot.

After all the men had been corralled, the women and children were told to go to the Public Parks where an armed guard would protect them and that a guard would protect their homes.

This ended the Riot so far as the Negro had anything to do with it.

Then came the great unthinkable, unspeakable climax. The White people went into those homes just vacated, carried away everything of value, opened safes, destroyed all legal papers and documents, then set fire to the buildings to hide their crime.

Then, not satisfied with the result, they framed charges against every leading Negro in an attempt to jail them and to intimidate the others, saying that the whole fault lay with the educated Negroes.

The fact is that the educated Negroes have never caused trouble or friction, but there has been allowed to flourish a crowd of uneducated Whites and Negroes who lived by their wits, and it is the intermingling of these Whites with these

Negroes that has always been the starting point of most of
our trouble.

P. S. Thompson, Ph.C.
Pres. Tulsa Medical,
Dental & Pharmaceutical Assn.

»«

TULSA, OKLA., JUNE 22, 1921

Causes: Race prejudices and the national lack of confidence
in law enforcement. This lack of confidence in law enforcement causes the Negro to feel that it is necessary to protect
himself in most cases of threatened lynching. If the party is
a member of our group he is most generally lynched, even
though promised the assurance of protection by law, and if
of the other group, he is not lynched if given such protection.

The lynchers often not only get the guilty parties but wreak
vengeance upon the innocent as well. Hence, the circulation
of a report of lynching of members of our group is a signal
to get ready for self-defense. It's like a spark in gasoline, it is
generally uncontrollable and does not require leadership to
mass its forces. But it often requires cool heads to prevent
a conflagration and catastrophe. This was even employed in
the Tulsa Riot.

First the report of lynching, the signal to arms, the promise of protection, the rapid spreading of lawlessness, the
cooler heads failing to act with sufficient alacrity to prevent
the catastrophe.

Shortly after daylight on Wednesday, June 1, 1921, I received a call to come to the hospital to dress two wounded men. I dressed hurriedly and started to the hospital. Just as I opened my front door a shot was fired at me from a nearby hill, the bullet grazed my leg. I shut the door. A few moments later my wife, hearing the shots, slightly opened the door and a second volley was fired. At this time the shots struck the porch. We shut the door and my wife said, "Doctor, let us go, our lives are worth more than everything." I sat my cases down in the hall and my wife and niece hurriedly dressed, locked the house and departed.

Shortly after we left a whistle blew. The shots rang from a machine gun located on the Stand Pipe Hill near my residence and aeroplanes began to fly over us, in some instances very low to the ground. A cry was heard from the women saying, "Look out for the aeroplanes, they are shooting upon us." The shots continued to be fired in rapid succession from high-powered guns from the vicinity of the hill. We continued to flee until we were about two miles northeast of the city. There we tarried at the home of a friend. Shortly the fire broke out, the bullets continued to whistle. The fire grew rapidly, we saw it spreading over our entire district south of the hill.

About 10 o'clock men came out in cars and told us the troops had come. Shortly afterwards we saw men dressed as soldiers in automobiles rounding up the people and asking them to go back, that they were safe, and on our return my wife and niece were told to go up Greenwood Street and I was searched and told to go in another direction to

Convention Hall, where I was marched with hands up and hat off. I was searched with hands up by two or three different sets of officers. I reached Convention Hall about 10:30. On the way to Convention Hall, possibly thirty minutes after the troops came, there was only one small fire north of the hill, but the next day when I viewed the devastated area, there were hundreds of houses burned after the troops had rounded up the men and taken them to Convention Hall.

I remained at the Convention Hall until I was released and sent with a Red Cross worker and the County Physician to the Morning Side Hospital to assist in treating the wounded in company with the County Physician. I came by my home to see if it was destroyed and to get my medicine cases.

On reaching the house I saw my piano and all of my elegant furniture piled in the street. My safe had been broken open, all of the money stolen, also my silverware, cut glass, all of the family clothing, and everything of value had been removed, even my family Bible. My electric light fixtures were broken, all the window lights and glass in the doors were broken, the dishes that were not stolen were broken, the floors were covered (literally speaking) with glass, even the phone was torn from the wall. In the basement we gathered two tubs of broken glass from off the floor. My car was stolen and most of my large rugs were taken. I lost seventeen houses that paid me an average of over $425.00 per month.

I worked heroically for the Red Cross and being the Assistant County Physician my work was doubly hard. For the first three days I did not stop to clean up my house, save moving my furniture onto the porch. I worked extremely hard for three or four days after the Riot, I almost collapsed. We slept out at the Fair Grounds, the first night without any bed, on the hard floor; spent the next night or two at the schoolhouse, then we came home and slept in the house with the doors broken and the window lights out. In the meantime I was assigned to a sanitarium, where the slightly wounded were treated. I dressed a number of cases without any assistance, in the meantime answering a number of calls out in the city for the Red Cross.

About the fourth night after the riot I received a call to go to the Fair Grounds, where a large number of Negro refugees were assembled. My wife, being nervous and suffering other infirmities as a result of the Riot, urged me to stay with her as she was seriously sick. I asked to be excused as I had already made two calls that same evening. The next night I was asked to go to the Fair Grounds, not having sufficiently recovered my strength and doing heavy work during the day I asked them to see if they could not get another doctor in my stead, so they found one. I continued to work at this sanitarium for the slightly wounded and also treated cases in the city. To my surprise, about a week or ten days later I saw statements in the paper that I refused to work with the Red Cross without pay. And the White Medical Association voted to discontinue an allowance of $25.00 per week for the above reason. A day before this, however, I was given the credit of leading a riot two years ago; going up to the police station and demanding to see if a certain prisoner was safe who was threatened to be lynched. Of this occurrence I knew nothing at the time it happened until the next morning and for two years after this said event occurred. Although many were quite familiar with it, my name was never mentioned.

It seems that several things have been said and done to discredit and to kill the influence of the men who have large holdings in this burned district.

Dr. R. T. Bridgewater
Assistant County Physician

>«

Fourteen Years in Tulsa

TULSA, OKLA., JUNE 22, 1921

In these years I have noticed a growing racial hate by the lower Whites because of Negro prosperity and independence; also a racial hatred because of Negro rooming house porters, whom they claim associated with White women in these places. Of this hate Yellow Journalism was mostly responsible in promoting.

Next, lax law enforcement by both county and city. The lawless element of both races were so arrogant that it was dangerous for the best citizens to make much protest. The "Chock" joint evil being of the worst type of breeding places for lawlessness, where White and Colored of their kind met and socialized. These forces reached the place of unrestraint, broke loose on a pretense, and thus swept down upon the good citizen with all the hate and revenge that has been smoldering for years. So the innocent suffered most, who thought little of their homes being burned.

Most people, like myself, stayed in their homes, expecting momentarily to be given protection by the Home Guards or State Troops, but instead of protection by the Home Guards they (the Home Guards) joined in with the hoodlums in shooting in good citizens' homes. This was my experience, so after seeing no protection from them, I took my family and a few friends in my car and drove four miles into the country where we were gathered up by State Troops who were perfect gentlemen and treated us like citizens of real America.

E. A. Loupe
Plumber

»«

TULSA, OKLA., JUNE 23, 1921

About 9:30 on the night of Tuesday, May 31, 1921, I heard the report of guns and thought it a fire signal. Then I found out what the trouble was. I became tangled up with the walls of my bed room and after getting straightened out I went to the door, saw people rushing to and fro. I called to a man and asked what the trouble was and finally my neighbor told me that the White people were going to lynch a man. I dressed the little girl who was with me at the time and went to a neighbor, stayed there until about one o'clock and then returned home. I tried to sleep but could not, so arose about 4:30 Wednesday A.M. and saw people rushing from

Greenwood and that section of the town. A group of Whites, stationed on the hill, fired upon them, some falling, others struggling on to safety. Then it dawned upon me of the danger of my invalid mother who has been helpless for four years. She was about six blocks from me up in the direction from which the people were fleeing.

I reached her in the midst of a rain of bullets. My sisters and I gathered her up, placed her on a cot and three of us carried the cot and the other one carried a bundle of clothes; thus we carried mother about six blocks, with bullets falling on all sides. About six squads of rioters overtook us, asked for men and guns, made us hold up our hands. There were boys in the bunch from about 10 years upward, all armed with guns. They would go into the houses, take what they wanted and then burn the house.

Our men were all disarmed as soon as caught. About 11 o'clock the enemy took my invalid mother and one of my sisters, supposedly to send them to Convention Hall for safety. Another sister and I scouted about until one o'clock when along came a truck and picked me up and carried me to Convention Hall, where I stayed until about 2 o'clock. On entering Convention Hall I failed to find my mother so I went in search for her. With the aid of the Red Cross I found her that night at the North Methodist Church. I made myself contented until Thursday and came out to see if I had a home. Out of three houses that had brought me $45.00 per month rent, I found one little rickety shack. After finding it I returned for my mother, kept her until Sunday morning, and in the meantime I tried to get a pass to send her away but failed to get one, so I took what little change I had left and sent her away. She remained unconscious for two weeks and then passed away. When we were trying to take her to safety an aeroplane shot down a man right in our path.

I feel that this damnable affair has ruined us all.

Mrs. Carrie Kinlaw

»«

TULSA, OKLA., JUNE 23, 1921

On the night of the Riot I was living at 623 Hill Street. My wife was sick, having been confined only three days. She was under the care of Dr. Jackson, who was to have called the next morning at 8 o'clock. I heard the firing all night. In the early morning the Whites began firing on my house so I had to try to find a place of safety to take my wife. When I returned my children had taken her to a neighbor's home. By that time they were looting and burning my home. We had two large trunks which they took into the street and burst open, took what they wanted and set fire to the rest.

The rest of my family with my wife made it to the soldiers for protection. She was so sick that she fainted. They had me surrounded so I got a water barrel, rolled it into an orchard of peach trees and hid in it until the storm passed over.

I lost about $2,500 worth of property.

J. P. Hughs

»«

TULSA, OKLA., JUNE 24, 1921

I was living on Williams Street and was at home on the night of the 31st. I went on the street and met about seven women running for refuge from Archer and Greenwood Streets and that section of the town. I watched over them at my home throughout the night. When morning came and the firing started they again ran for safety, leaving my wife, three children—a baby and two elder children—and myself. I continued to watch over my family until about 8 o'clock A.M., when the two elder children, a girl and boy, fled northward for safety, leaving my wife, baby and me. My wife not being well, I remained at home amid the shower of bullets from the hill. We opened the house, raised the curtains and shades and stayed in sight as near as possible amid the bullets—we would appear on the porch. To the best of my ability I kept all males from the house. Then a bunch of Whites came down from the hill. My wife and I ventured out amidst the volley of fire, met them about a block from home and told them that my wife was sick and I did not want to leave her. They had me raise my hands and searched me. I was bareheaded—one did not want me to even get my hat, but my wife threw it to me. The Lieutenant who was leading them assured me that my wife and baby would be safe and that my home would not be molested. Then I was marched to the top of the brick yard hill and there I was called all kinds of names by boys from 10 years to men of 60. Then I was loaded on a truck and carried to the corner of Boulder and Brady Streets and here I was taken off the truck and searched again, cursed, called all kinds of names in the language of "Take your hat off," "Throw up your hands," "Be submissive and obey to the letter." Even boys of 10. I obeyed.

After entering Convention Hall I met with very courteous treatment because I was well known among the better class of Whites. In the meantime my wife and I were separated. They took her and baby to the park, she being sick. I was in a fit of eagerness to find her so I phoned the man by whom I was employed and he came and got me released, took me in a truck and went in search of my wife. At the Baseball Park I found that my daughter had fallen into an epileptic fit and was sent to a hospital.

In a frenzy of despair my task had just begun, but by the help of the "God send" Red Cross answering my wants as far as first aid to the body, but no satisfaction of the mind. I found my wife and baby safe at the Fifth Street Methodist Church.

If we had had complete co-operation from the officers of Tulsa they could have prevented all this disaster, and not use the occasion to demoralize our business industries and our nice homes, but instead of protection it was seemingly a matter of destroy and abolish all Negro business and nice residences.

A. J. Newman

»«

TULSA, OKLA., JUNE 24, 1921

On Tuesday evening we heard the shooting and several friends came to my home for shelter until about 2 o'clock. Then in the early morning the Whites were stationed on the hill with machine guns and high-powered rifles, firing upon our people as they tried to run for safety.

About seven o'clock the Whites or Home Guards came for the men. Then they took the women and children, promising them safety. After they had the homes vacated one bunch of whites would come in and loot. Even women with shopping bags would come in, open drawers, take every kind of finery from clothing to silverware and jewelry. Men were carrying out the furniture, cursing as they did so, saying, "These d— Negroes have better things than lots of white people." I stayed until my home was caught on fire, then I ran to the hill side where there were throngs of White people; women, men and children, even babies, watching and taking snap shots of the proceedings of the mob. Some remarked that "The city ought to be sued for selling D— niggers property so close to the city." One woman noticed the First Baptist Church, which is a beautiful structure located near a White residence district. She said, "Yonder is a nigger church, why ain't they burning it?" The reply was, "It's in a White district."

I saw an old Colored man, Mr. Oliver, who stayed with Dr. Jackson. I hailed him and asked him to help me with my handbag. He told me that Dr. Jackson was killed with his hands up. He said the ruffians ordered him out of his beautiful home. He came out with his hands up and said, "Here

I am boys, don't shoot," but they shot him just the same. About this time some Home Guards appeared and ordered Mr. Oliver to come to them. While doing so a bunch of rifles were raised to shoot. The Guards fell down and Mr. Oliver took shelter behind a post just in time to save his life. Then Mr. Oliver went to the Guards and they searched him, with hands up, and took over $50.00 from him, which they failed to return, and then took him to Convention Hall.

Then the horde of ruffians went down on Detroit, looting those beautiful homes of everything then burned them, even breaking the phones from the walls. The machine guns just shattered the walls of the homes. The fire department came out and protected the White homes on the west side of Detroit Street while on the east side of the street men with torches and women with shopping bags continued their looting and burning of Negro homes, while aeroplanes flew overhead, some very low.

I watched this awful destruction from where I sat on the hill side. As I sat watching my modern 10-room and basement home burn to ashes an old White man came by. Addressing me as "Auntie," he said, "It's awful, ain't it?" and offered me a dollar to buy my dinner with.

Name withheld by request

»«

TULSA, OKLA., JUNE 24, 1921

On the morning of June 1st, I met the mob of Whites at the door where I was. They marched me to Convention Hall with my hands up. From there I was taken to the Ball Park and saw many men and women who were homeless. There I slept on two benches.

I left the park the next morning and looked up my wife who was stopping with some friends. Then I purchased a folding chair, a strop and razor and went down on Greenwood amidst the ashes and ruins and started a barber shop.

From a 10-room and basement modern brick home, I am now living in what was my coal barn. From a 5-chair white enamel barber shop, 4 baths, electric clippers, electric fan, 2 lavatories and shampoo stands, 4 workmen, double marble shine stand, a porter and an income of over $500 or $600 per month, to a razor, strop and folding chair on the sidewalk.

I feel that corrupt politics is the cause of the whole affair, for if the authorities had taken the proper steps in time the whole matter could have been prevented.

C. L. Netherland
Proprietor of a Barber Shop

»«

TULSA, OKLA., JUNE 22, 1921

TO WHOM IT MAY CONCERN: The catastrophe that occurred at Tulsa on the night of May 31, 1921, to June 1, 1921, was outrageous. It was heinous and beyond our ability to describe, but we have been asked to give our opinion.

Being very busy at our office we did not turn our attention

to any of the rumors that were being circulated about an attempted plan to lynch the boy who was supposed to be the accused party of an attempted assault upon a White girl, as the story goes.

On Wednesday, the 1st of June, about the hour in the early morning when the battle was hot, I stood at my window in my room and saw White guards (Home Guards) break into stores of all kinds and carry out the contents that were being loaded onto trucks, then hastened towards the White district of the city. We are very much of the opinion that some of these groceries and dry goods are being sold to us now by various White hucksters.

When we were taken to the Convention Hall we were treated very fair. Our opinion is that the affair could have been averted had the better class of Whites and Negroes gotten together and adjusted affairs.

We do not wish to be radical, as a large number of White dailies and pulpits have been in placing the blame. They have based their argument on racial equality, which the Negro has never hoped for nor worked for. Let us, therefore, refrain from such lambast.

Racial equality only means equal manhood and womanhood. The solution, in our minds, is "Let the Negro obey the Ten Commandments and the White man the Golden Rule, then Ephriam will not vex Judas and Judas will not vex Ephriam." We are not giving our full opinion at this writing as we are preparing a personal pamphlet that will deal with all classes of the Riot which occurred here. We are unable to say at this writing when it will be ready.

M. D. Russell
Exchange Ins. Co.

>«

On Tuesday evening, May 31st, 1921, I was called and told of some mail that was at 500. N. Detroit Ave. When I reached this point I was told of the differences between the two races. Then it was beginning to get warm, which made it dangerous for me to return to my home in the Addition, so I remained on Detroit Ave. all night.

I saw people of all descriptions going up and down the street, and most of them were armed. Early in the morning, between 5 and 6 A.M., a "Riot Call" was given; that is, the City whistle gave one long blow and then looking through the windows I could see the Whites, armed with high-powered rifles, coming from the hill and surrounding the Colored district. As they filed past and called into the houses for the people to come out, I said that "I would wait as long as possible." They would say, "Come out, we are not going to hurt you." Several people responded to the call, but I would look cooly on as they marched others away.

Viewing the rear of the house I could see men and boys swarming around the Colored people's homes, while others looted and burned the homes of my people. Watching with my two companions at how my people were treated, it occurred to me to remain there as long as possible, which I did.

After seeing most of the property that was near me burned, I surrendered with my companions, knowing that all windows and doors had been shot out and it fell to our lot to come out.

On the arrival of the bunch of Whites, the fourth or fifth time we came out after several shots were fired into the house by the mob. We came out, my companions first. Two or three Whites thrust guns in each man's face and side and took him down stairs. As I neared the bottom of the steps I was met by a man who very unkindly treated me. Seeing a man with hands raised he came up to the blind side and struck me in the jaw. Did I see him? NO! After which I was questioned and my money taken and then for a ride through the busy streets, with hands raised, for about thirty blocks.

On the way my arms got tired and, too, the sun was baking my brains, as I was not permitted to get my hat. I lowered my hands to keep off the sun and was struck on the hands with a gun and told to "Put them up." While riding through the streets, women and children, and very often men, would laugh and make merry.

After getting to the Park, the women were permitted to take the grandstand, while the men were clustering around on the grounds. Later they were permitted to go to the grandstand, those from 50 years and upwards, while there was plenty of room for all.

Then came the unpleasant duty of getting out. You must have some White person to vouch for you, and, of course, I did not know anyone (being an architect, my brother and I have contracted and worked for ourselves). So I was up against a hard proposition, but finally I got out through a young fellow who told a man that "This boy is my brother-in-law."

On returning home the house had been ransacked, two or more of the mob changing clothes. One piece they had changed had been worn about four times. Can you imagine what that fact, alone, brings out?

The worst thing of all was being humiliated before little boys between the ages of 12 and 16 years, so you know it will grow up in the youngsters to try the same thing when he has matured, that others tried, but with less success, I am hoping.

J. C. Latimer
Architect and Contractor

»«

One of the most horrible scenes of race hatred and Tuesday, May 31st, and morning of Wednesday, June 1st, mob violence occurred at Tulsa, Okla., on the night of that history has ever recorded on the face of the globe.

This sad occurrence committed by more than 5,000 Whites has blackened the city of Tulsa's character and placed a black stain upon this great Oil City that can never be erased, I happened to note, being a resident of Tulsa.

The *Daily Tribune*, a White newspaper that tries to gain its popularity by referring to the Negro settlement as "Little Africa," came out on the evening of Tuesday, May 31, with an article claiming that a Negro had had some trouble with a White elevator girl at the Drexel Bldg. It also said that the

Negro had been arrested and placed in jail and that a mob of Whites were forming in order to lynch the Negro.

Sometime during the night about 50 Negroes arrived; then scores with rifles, etc., went up to the district where the accused Negro was in prison, and upon their arrival, found a host of Whites who were making an effort to lynch the Negro.

The Negroes were given the assurance by officials in charge that no lynching would take place, and as they were about to return to the Negro section, someone fired a shot and the battle began. All night long they could be heard firing from both sides, while the Whites were marshalling more than 5,000 men who had surrounded the Negro section to make an early attack in the morning on more than 8,000 innocent Negroes.

As daylight approached, they (the Whites) were given a signal by a whistle, and the dirty, cowardly outrage took place. All of this happened while innocent Negroes were slumbering, and did not have the least idea that they would fall victims of such brutality.

At the signal of the whistle, more than a dozen aeroplanes went up and began to drop turpentine balls upon the Negro residences, while the 5,000 Whites, with machine guns and other deadly weapons, began firing in all directions. Negro men, women and children began making haste to flee to safety, but to no avail, as they were met on all sides with volleys of shot. Negro men, women and children were killed in great numbers as they ran, trying to flee to safety.

As the fighting progressed they were capturing and taking all Negro men from their honest homes to a down town hall, etc., also Negro women and children were being taken to different parts of the city. After they had cleared more than five hundred homes of occupants, then the dirty work of firing and looting of homes began.

Torch lights were used with gasoline to burn up the Negro settlement, and, in the meantime, they used large trucks to load up pianos, victrolas and other articles that were in the Negro homes. In fact, the whole of the Negro homes were looted by these rascal Whites who met no resistance, as most of the Negroes were taken prisoners.

We read the Bible about Sodom and Gomorrah, but the sights, as witnessed that morning, could not have been worse. One part of the city was cut off from the other by fire, smoke and ashes.

The most horrible scenes of this occurrence were to see women dragging their children while running to safety, and the dirty White rascals firing at them as they ran. Some of them were pursued more than 12 or 15 miles, and some have never returned.

Negro hospitals, with numbers of sick, were burned, and many people perished in the flames, not being able to get to a place of safety.

Tulsa, in which many Negroes had accumulated much wealth and fine homes, and Greenwood Street, the Negroes' "Broadway" of Tulsa and one of the best Negro business streets in the whole U.S.A., now lies a heap of ashes. As the debris was being cleared away, bodies were found buried, burned to a crisp. They had had no means of escape.

The number of Whites and Negroes killed in this raid will never be known. I was detained at the police station to assist the White and Colored doctors with wounded Negroes, and all day long, from early morning until night, truck loads of Negroes were being brought by, dead and wounded. Where they were taken, I don't know.

Several Negroes were tied to the backs of automobiles, and dragged through the streets while bullets were being fired into their bodies.

Women were being chased from their homes naked, with clothes in their hands and volleys of shots fired at them as they were fleeing; some with babies in their arms.

These things, and many others, which I will not be able to mention, were done in America, which makes its boast of true democracy.

Oh, America! Cruel America! Thou art weighed in the balance.

A. H.

>«

Tulsa Race Riot

It is impossible to make a full report of the happenings, but what I saw was bad enough, and yet I cannot tell all that I saw. When I fully realized what was happening I saw men and women fleeing for their lives, with White men by the hundreds pursuing them, firing in all directions. As one woman was running from her home she suddenly fell with a bullet wound. Then I saw aeroplanes, as they flew very low. To my surprise, as they passed over the business district they left the entire block a mass of flame.

I saw men, women and children driven like cattle, huddled like horses and treated like beasts. Thus, I fully realized the attitude of the Southern White man when he has you bested. I saw hundreds of men marched through the main business section of "White Town" with their hats off and their hands up, with dozens of guards marching them with guns, cursing them for everything mentionable. I saw large trucks following up the invaders, as they ran the Colored people from their homes and places of business. Everything of value was loaded on these trucks and everything left was burned to ashes.

I saw machine guns turned on the Colored men to oust them from their stronghold.

Tuesday night, May 31st, was the riot, and Wednesday morning, by daybreak, was the invasion.

»«

H. T. S. JOHNSON, OF THE INTER-RACIAL COMMISSION

The race riot in Tulsa, on the night of May 31st, and the murder and arson on the morning of June 1st, 1921, never would have happened had the better class of White people and Negroes been working co-operatively for community good. Instead, each went his way, giving no thought as to what would become of any community where the right-thinking people leave the running of things municipal in the hands of persons who value money more than they do law and order government.

An awful price—hundreds of lives and millions in property—has been paid, but if the Christian people of both race groups have learned the lesson that, for mutual protection and community welfare, they must concern themselves about the character of city officials, from mayor to the humblest policeman, the investment is worthwhile. If not fully, the writer believes the lesson has been sufficiently learned to make, forever impossible, a recurrence of the tragedy which makes every loyal Tulsan blush for shame when occasion arises to remember it.

The best evidence that the above is true was the organizing, within less than thirty days after the disaster, of two committees on inter-racial co-operation. One, composed of a group of influential and fair-minded White people, and the other of a no less representative group of Negroes. These committees met a public sentiment on both sides that was a mixture of hatred, suspicion and sympathy. The element of sympathy, however, was more pronounced among the ——es of both groups, and that was the leverage with which the White inter-racial committee lifted the lid of Negro oppression upon which the city administration sat with all the weight that politics and graft courts command. In other words, to prevent Negroes from building back their homes and business places, the city commissioners, two days after their district was burned, passed an ordinance extending the fire limits far enough north and west to include all the land which certain interests coveted, as Ahab did Naboth's vineyard. After refusing to heed his plea that they rescind the confiscatory fire ordinance, Judge Mather M. Eakes, chairman of the Tulsa County Commission on Inter-Racial Co-operation (White), in a law suit against the city, —— the fire ordinance unconstitutional, and thus left the Negroes free to rebuild on the lots for which they held deeds. Without this timely aid, the Negro's morale would have broken and the splendid record in rebuilding and re-establishing business, which he is now making, would have been impossible.

Better sanitation, more lights, paved streets, more and better equipped school buildings, ample play grounds and equipment for same, gymnasiums, a swimming pool, and a library with a paid attendant are our most pressing needs. With a strong Negro committee to make an intelligent survey and an influential White committee to press our claim with existent authorities, in due time we should have the things enumerated above and a greater and better Tulsa will have emerged from the blood and ashes of June 1st. Truly inter-racial co-operation is the way to peace in race relations.

>«

MRS. DORA WELLS

Too much cannot be said about this noble woman and her great work in Tulsa during the great disaster of June 1st, 1921. Mrs. Wells, although a widow and a sufferer of heavy losses herself, never faltered in her work. She administered to the sick, fed many hungry persons. Able only to build three small rooms, for many nights she gave shelter to several people. Before the disaster Mrs. Wells was owner and proprietor of the Wells Garment Factory, an establishment that gave employment to several race women. Leaving a home and business, with every comfort of life in them, only to come back June 2nd to find smoldering embers and ashes—the work of a lifetime gone. Although crushed, but not conquered, this woman set to work to erect a temporary building of three rooms, being the first person to erect a frame building in the much coveted district.

Mrs. Wells left Tulsa, August 20, 1921, as a delegate to the Elks Grand Lodge and Temple of I.B.P.O.E.W., held in Boston, Mass. Being an ardent church and society worker, Mrs. Wells was able to put the condition of Tulsa sufferers before that Grand body. By so doing she received clothing from the Temples in the East; also two churches and two clubs responded. Two hundred and sixty-seven persons were given clothing from the bundles from this noble woman's hand, assisted by the members of Daughter Elks of Cosmopolitan Temple 133, of Tulsa. Persons who needed help most received it, regardless of their fraternal connections. All were treated alike, and today, no one receives more hospitality than those who visit Mrs. Wells. Her table is always ready to feed the hungry, her roof to shelter the homeless. Tulsa can well be proud of such a woman. Loved by all, feared by none, women of her all-around serviceable and resourceful type are not found in great numbers, and Tulsa should be proud of her.

The people of Tulsa who benefited by her assistance shall never forget her services rendered in a time of need.

Several cash donations were sent from various Temples, which was divided by her among daughter Elk only.

>»«

After eleven months have passed and I have had the pleasure of seeing beautiful Greenwood re-built with two- and three-story business structures, I want to forget that morning of June 1, when I tried to find a hiding place, and there was no place to hide. When we left the Red Wing Hotel (husband and I), bullets were falling like rain, and I resigned myself to my fate for I felt that all avenues of escape were cut off.

Mr. Pack and Lewis called to my husband to bring me out and try to get out of range of the fire and bullets. When I reached the street I became sick and so weak in my knees I could not walk.

There was a man in a taxi trying to help the women escape. He took us in and drove us as far as 1025 North Greenwood. We had friends living there and thought we could stop there, but, alas! we found in a few minutes we would have to go further on, as by that time they were firing on us there.

With Mr. Harris and his family and many others, we started out walking north, but where? We did not know. However, there were about six aeroplanes keeping watch overhead. For what?

When we reached the section line, Mr. Pack and my husband decided it would be best for us to try and get to the Kennedy Building where my husband worked. I would not dare repeat all we heard en route, but when we reached Main and Archer they were trotting a large bunch of our men to Convention Hall, hands held over their heads, bare headed and half clad. The streets were lined with White people, some in pity for the unfortunate, but the majority seemed to think it a funny thing to do.

We reached the Kennedy Building and were taken care of there for the day. When evening came, they had decided we could go on the streets, but must wear a tag on which was printed "Police Protection." Anyone without a tag would be arrested.

The days that followed brought many humiliations. If you had never worked in service you must have a card showing you were in the Red Cross Service or some responsible White person's employment. Guards stationed all about you must show a "Green Card" before you could enter the Colored district.

I am now employed as secretary at Maurice Willows Hospital and find on file a list of names, very incomplete, as follows: Colored wounded 63; Dead, 15.

This report cannot be relied upon as correct.

We dismissed our last Riot patient on April 28, a young man that has suffered much and who is still on crutches.

Let us hope we can forgive and forget those of whatever race that caused such a catastrophe to befall us. Make our lives an example for others, as law-abiding, Christian people, saying, "Father, forgive them, for they know not what they do."

>«

Things I noticed while trying to escape:

Mother and son, both wounded, one trying to help the other.

Several men wounded, on the side of the road, exhausted, unable to go farther.

Have been informed by nurses that they had several premature births on that day.

Children frantically trying to find parents; wives waiting for husbands, not knowing where they had been taken when the armed men took them away.

To all American citizens everywhere I will say, "Talk against all lawlessness."

Dimple L. Bush

>«

History of Mt. Zion Baptist Church

The Mt. Zion Baptist Church of Tulsa, Okla., was organized in the year 1909 by the late S. Lyons with a small group. He pastored this people about eight months and resigned. Rev. Leonard was then called to the pastorage of the church. He only stayed a short time, and then Rev. C. L. Netherland, the third pastor, filled his place as pastor of this little flock for about eighteen months, then stepped aside and encouraged them to call Rev. F. K. White, who was the fourth pastor and prime mover of the buying of the present site where the church now stands. Rev. White left them in the year 1914 for California. Before leaving he persuaded them to elect R. A. Whitaker, the present pastor, who came in the darkest hours when odds were all against us.

At that time we were worshipping in the school house on Hartford, and in less than three months after my arrival we were ordered to vacate. This we did with a three days' notice. We moved in a "dance hall" in the Woods Building, on Greenwood Avenue. It was there that friend and foe said that the day of hope had passed and it was then that we went boldly to a "Shrine of Grace" and God opened the door through Brother C. Henry, who came to our relief with a message of hope.

The next move was the "Tabernacle" building and the breaking of the ground for the new church site. This will show you where we were seven years ago. We started the "land breaking" without a penny.

Five years ago in June we had a big rally and raised seven hundred and fifteen dollars and fifteen cents. With this we started the work on the foundation of the present building. We had to build up a credit, and work by chances. This was a hard task, as we had plenty of knockers, but we soon found that every knock was a boost. We had a good standing with the following business firms: Ketchum Lumber Company, Miller Furniture Company, Tulsa Brick Company, as well as with our own members and friends, Brother J. H. Goodwin, Mrs. M. A. Wright, Mrs. Ida Grant, Mrs. M. Littles, J. Woods, J. E. Stewart, A. Allis, J. W. Franklin and many others whose names I cannot call.

We give you this bit of history so you will understand what seven years of toil in a field where conditions and odds are against one means.

We thank the many friends who stayed with us and gave us words of cheer. God bless the good people of Tulsa and the great state of Oklahoma. We have gained many friends of the other races. We shall never forget you and pray the blessings of God upon you. This is our prayer.

R. A. Whitaker
Pastor

>«

Leaving Tulsa, as I did, on May 26, 1921, to be present at the graduation of my two daughters, Ruth and Eunice, the latter from the eighth grade, May 27, and the former from Western University, June 2, found me away from Tulsa on the dates of the riot, May 31 and June 1.

But the Tulsa that I left and the Tulsa that I found on my return, June 5!

I left a Tulsa throbbing with life and high hopes, people who were happy, people who in the main were prosperous, a wide awake, alert, active, forward-looking folk. Some who had come in the early day when it tried men's souls, and now were resting and beginning to enjoy the fruits of their years of toil—people who were singing the praises of Tulsa, prosperous.

No man, be he millionaire or pauper, had more pride in Tulsa than her upstanding, forward-looking colored citizens. None clamored harder against the overbearing police system and the evils of the underworld.

Ten months in Tulsa; ten active, constructive months of human hopes and aspirations; ten months of a vision of a better day and then on platform and in press the phrase, "The Dawn of a New Day," was in actual use. This in Tulsa, colored.

Tulsa's colored citizens settled in the north end of the city, separating themselves at right angles to the Tulsa white.

Standpipe Hill jutted out into the colored section like the state of Florida extends into the ocean. This hill is owned by a white man. From it one can get a fine panoramic view of Tulsa and the surrounding country. The white people would not buy it, and the colored could not, although they lived on three sides of it.

The good people of color were building magnificent church structures. One, Mt. Zion Baptist, had merged into completion at a cost of $85,000—hard-earned and frugally kept. It was a consolation to the old members who had labored many years and now, in a home comfortable, were ready to worship God and patiently serve until He called them home.

Paradise Baptist Church was a cozy brick building situated on the north side of Standpipe Hill, while Mt. Zion was on the south side of it. The members of this church were building on the pay-as-you-go plan. It was completed with the exception of interior furnishings. The Methodist Episcopal churches had their first story completed and money in the bank for the superstructure.

There were four well equipped drug stores, many grocery stores. Elliott & Hooker, men's and women's furnishing store, carried as high a grade of goods as any in the city; two fine hotels accommodated the traveling public; Welcome grocery was a model; modern barber shops, and two shoe shops with up-to-date machinery. Dreamland Theatre catered to the pleasure and entertainment of the people. The physicians were equipping themselves with all the modern apparatus required to alleviate human suffering. Young men as dentists had invested heavily in preparing to take care of the distressed in their line. Women had invested in beauty parlors and dressmaking establishments. Cafes were prepared to feed satisfactorily the many patrons. In fact, the people were so industrious and put in so much time at work that they did not prepare their food at home, but patronized the cafes. Four upholstered jitney busses carried the people from their homes to their work. An undertaking establishment equipped with caskets ranging from $50 to $1,000, all for the accommodation of the colored people. A $10,000 limousine for the accommodation of the bereaved families was the latest addition.

The Tulsa colored people, in every sense of the word, were building a modern, up-to-date business city.

They were constantly handicapped as to public utilities, which were managed and controlled by the white man.

They constantly prayed him to extend and furnish the same. Procrastination, political promises and hope deferred was the final result. The colored section of Tulsa was insufficiently lighted. And if evil did hold sway and the bad Negro did exist he had the cover of a neglected city darkness to ply his evil trade. They have cried, "Let there be light," and there was no light. The kerosene lamp, the tallow dip or darkness prevailed in their city. In Tulsa, white night had been turned into day.

The unsanitary condition, the surface tub-toilets and the stench therefrom increased the wonder that the health of the community was as good as it was.

The colored man of Tulsa built his home not upon sand, but upon an exceedingly great faith, for when fire does break out all he can do is to stand by and see all his earthly possessions go down in ashes. Water protection was insufficient.

In spite of all the physical and mental handicaps he has wrought well, and though a part of his city lies in ashes, the carpenter's hammer is heard and new lumber in the form of a house flares up in every direction. The Tulsa attitude of the black man is to build and rebuild.

The Young Men's Christian Association was the latest addition to civic betterment. This is an inspiring chapter in the city's history.

Conscious of the unwholesome moral trend of the life of the young people, a few active, wide-awake, progressive citizens, on their own initiative and the friendly counsel and co-operation of that fine Christian gentleman, Mr. C. E.

Buckner, general secretary of the Tulsa "Y," set about the organization of the Hunton Branch Y.M.C.A.

They raised their own budget of $3,012 for the first year's work. The central association stood ready to furnish $1,000 of it, but the board of managers, led on by that prince of men, Mr. S. D. Hooker, raised the full amount themselves. The membership was more than 500 men and boys.

In like manner they raised the budget for the next year's work and, notwithstanding the tightness of the times, they increased the budget to $5,207 and had the pleasure on Tuesday evening, before the Tuesday of the riot, of rejoicing over the fact that the entire amount had been pledged.

Shortly before that a community institute was held. For the first time in the history of the University of Oklahoma, the Extension Division, consisting of seven white men and women, experts in their lines, carried on a three-day session in the colored community of Tulsa. They touched and stimulated the church, school, civic and home life of the people in a most encouraging manner. It gave our people a new hold on the cheering possibilities of life. The workers were pleasantly informed as to the inner life and cravings of the colored people. The latter did not know that white people could be so kind, helpful and interested in their personal problems. The institute cost $1,000. The people thought it worth many times the cost.

These are some of the evidences of the new attitude of mind developing in Tulsa's colored citizens.

Just another fact showing the desire for civic improvement, wholesome ideals and better things for Tulsa.

Just a week before the riot, the board of managers of Hunton Branch Y.M.C.A., together with the mayor and city commissioners, invited President King, of the Republic of Liberia, to be Tulsa's guest. President King accepted.

This would have heartened the colored citizens of Oklahoma to make more of their opportunities. The $1,000 cost to the colored citizens of Tulsa for this visit of President King and his party was no deterrent.

The houses of Tulsa's colored citizens ranged from the temporary floorless box house to modern equipped ones of the latest and best interior and exterior furnishings.

This, in brief, and in brief only, for much can be said of the high hopes and aims of the colored citizens of Tulsa. This is the Tulsa that I left on the night of the 26th of May, 1921.

And the Tulsa that I found on my return the 4th of June. What a contrast!

Tulsa had turned a page to run parallel with the Huns and Goths—vandals of Europe or the Indians in Custer's last charge.

An awkward colored boy steps on the toe of a white elevator girl—she slaps him—a retort discourteous on his part—arrested on the charge of assault and battery—newspaper omits "and battery"—public thinks rape—threatening groups of whites gather about the jail—colored men, fearing the usual happening, gather to prevent a lynching—a careless, reckless shot—and the restraints of civilization are thrown aside and men became brutish beasts.

The boy ought to have apologized. The girl ought to have recognized the accident. The paper ought not to have garbled the story with false emphasis. White men ought not to have gathered about the jail. They should be willing to let the law have the right of way. The colored men ought to have trusted those whose sworn duty it was to protect the prisoner.

A cordon of police could have surrounded the first groups, white and black. But these are sad words, "It might have been." But nothing that happened can justify the driving of twelve thousand innocent, sleeping colored people, clad in their night clothes, out into the streets, marched to Convention Hall and elsewhere, then loot, rob and steal the hard, laborious earnings of a struggling people, handicapped at best.

I have worked ten months with these people. I have had a deep sympathy for them in their struggle against great odds.

Loot—they backed auto trucks up to the vacated (by force) Negro homes and loaded everything movable and of value. One colored woman went to eleven different white homes and in each recovered portions of her household goods.

Rob—every bit of money found on their persons was taken. Masonic rings were removed from their fingers, watches and chains from their persons. In fact, everything of a material nature, etc., preparatory to the cruel initiation which has not yet ended, was taken from them. And so, in their penniless, destitute condition, they were corralled, first one place and then another.

Thanks to the good people who took them into their homes, fed and clothed them, housed them until the cruel police order compelled even the white people to give up and send to the fair grounds those whom they had befriended. Kind offers were thwarted by the police regulation.

With homes looted, homes and stores burned to ashes, with the sick, aged and enfeebled carried out or left to perish in the flames; mothers giving birth to children in the open, herded, corralled and guarded like prisoners of war; and before the smoke of a thousand homes had blown away, the trembling homeless learn that the city fathers have passed an ordinance "making it forever impossible for them, in their destitute condition, to go back and rebuild on their own home place."

While their hearts are bleeding, their homes and all the relics that make the memory of life's past sustaining with shocking realization that their families are broken and scattered and fearing that they may be slain by the cruel bullet of the mob, with trembly, weak, tired, hungry and hungerless bodies, compelled to be in the stalls of the fair grounds under a heavy, cruel guard of home-guards—guards who greet them with harsh orders and vulgar language—while suffering all this and more, the mayor and commissioners, the Real Estate Exchange, the Welfare Board are like those who crucified Christ, casting lots for the Negro's hard-earned land.

Ah! if they would only stop and think how long it required for those poor, struggling people to own that little portion of earth!

Yet by every method known and being discovered by the combined trained minds of the best legal talent that the city and state affords, not one loop hole is being left through which or by means of which the colored citizen can ever again rebuild on his own land.

We appeal to the conscience and good judgment of the American people, where is the line separating the lower element that cleared the way and the higher element that sat at noon luncheon under the cool of the electric fans and carefully and judiciously planned that this "never again would be a Negro section."

And immediately proceeded to publish without the owner's consent or offering a cent:

"Wanted, Wholesale Houses in Tulsa."

"New Welfare Committee in active campaign to Better City."

"Through the Reconstruction Committee appointed by the Mayor and City Commissioners Tuesday (June 14), Tulsa extends a welcoming hand to wholesale houses and industrial plants which are to be located on the trackage property in Little Africa swept by fire and which is now within the city fire limits restricted to the erection of fire-resisting buildings."

"The committee also expressed a sentiment in favor of using a part of the burned area for a union station whenever such a project is ready for consideration by the railroads entering Tulsa."—*Tulsa World*, June 15, 1921.

Think of it! A union station where the races of men pass through, built upon the blood-stained soil of the Negroes' property. What an approach to Tulsa! What a gateway to the "Magic City of the Great Southwest." A symbol of greed and blood!

And added to that anguish of soul comes quick and fast the police regulation that all Negroes to have the freedom of Tulsa's streets must wear a green tag stating age, residence, name and name of employer, who must be white. Men who did business for themselves had to find a white man to sign their cards. If not employed, a red card must be worn. This reads, "If the bearer is on the streets after 7 o'clock he will be arrested and taken to the fair ground"—by some called the "bull-pen."

The guards are placed at all roads entering the colored section. Men, women, boys and girls are held up by these guards, many of whom are rough, rude and discourteous.

Every step from the sudden awakening by the firing of guns and the buzzing of aeroplanes to the present moment evidences in increasing humiliation. Those who were privileged to return to their homes found their contents gone or mutilated. Everything from a shoe to a piano to an automobile was found in the homes of white folks.

I left a happy, hopeful, progressive people. I found a crushed, humiliated, discouraged humanity. I left a praying people; I found them wondering if God is just. I left a Young Men's Christian Association with bright and promising prospects, just ready to jump into a $150,000 building campaign; I found a budget destroyed, resources consumed, a board of managers in despair.

Tulsa has destroyed the homes, taken the lives and maimed the bodies of the best friend the white man has in America; yea, the world.

There is no man in the world that has stood by and will stand by the white man like the Negro.

There is no justification for the wholesale destruction of property and resources of the thousands of innocent, law-abiding, home-building Negroes. We do not condone the wrong deeds of the bad Negro. We deplore his existence. We pray the co-operative influences of all people to help reform or restrain him as well as his co-partners in white. We find it difficult to reach him. You find it difficult to reach his white partner. They clash. You and we are thrown into a whirlpool of human rage. We, who emerge with bloody, bruised bodies, and the savings and buildings of a lifetime smoldering in ashes, must face each other and realize how trivial and avoidable the cause and how deplorable and lasting the results.

Is the spirit of America dead? Shall the color of a man's skin be the symbol for adverse sentiment?

Mine is a Christian program. Am thoroughly convinced that an active, wide-awake Christianity will cure this human ill.

There come times in a Christian program when it becomes necessary to "drive out the money changers," and land grafters.

Unhappily Tulsa has worked into that stage.

Tulsa is not all bad. There are good citizens in Tulsa. They, as much as any, deplore the spot that will not out.

We need a nearer approach to the principles and teaching of the Golden Rule. The hammer and claw, pistol and gun, create hate. And hate hurries us on to destruction.

There is no place in a Christian program for hate.

Let's make America safe for her own citizens and courteous to others.

>«

Tulsa's Separate School System

The separate school system of Tulsa is, perhaps, the most reliable standard by which we may judge the progress of its Negro citizens since it emerged from the "village" class. In spite of the fact that commercial Tulsa has grown in leaps and bounds almost "overnight," our separate school system has been able to keep pace with this rapid stride. When Tulsa loomed forth as the Negro metropolis of the South, prior to June the 1st, 1921, our schools maintained the same rank in the educational circles of the southland. Two schools, Dunbar and Washington, were built at a time when the increase in the Negro population of Tulsa was inestimable. Dunbar, an eight-room structure, had become inadequate and the overflow was being cared for in the Liberty school, in the northeast part of the city. Booker T. Washington, our high school, had grown from a four-room frame structure to a modern fifteen-room brick building. Eight brick unit buildings cared for the intermediate grades on the high school grounds. Thirty-nine teachers, representatives of the best colleges of the country, were employed to instruct the youth, and no teacher was employed who was not a graduate of an accredited school.

The grit and endurance of the Negroes of Tulsa since last June may well be determined by the progress of the schools since that time. Fifteen hundred children were enrolled in the schools last year. This year a little better than sixteen hundred are entered. Two extra units have been built on the high school grounds to take care of the increase in attendance. A fully equipped modern building of the latest type takes the place of Dunbar, which was burned. Eight units surround this building, and at present half-day sessions are being held to accomodate the children. Our high school is accredited for twenty-eight units, and its graduates are admitted to the best colleges of the country without examination. The science and commercial departments of this school are among the best of the South. Tulsa schools are keeping pace with Tulsa's growth, and Tulsa's growth has not been affected by recent unfortunate events.

>«

Where Are the Dead?

We have reached the point in the stream of time where every earnest hearted person should say, in the language of St. Paul,

"Let God be true, though it prove every man a liar." (Rom. 3:4.) Then let us settle the question according to the word of God. "The dead praise not the Lord, neither they that go down in silence." (Psa. 115:17.) "His (man's) breath goeth forth, he returns to the dust; in that very day his thoughts perish." (Psa. 145:4.) "For the living know that they shall die; but the dead know not anything, neither have they any more a reward; for the memory of them is forgotten. Also their love, and their hatred, and their envy is now perished; neither have they any more a portion forever of anything that is under the sun. Whatsoever thy hand findeth to do, do with thy might; for there is no work, nor device, nor knowledge, nor wisdom in the grave where thou goest." (Eccl. 9:5, 6, 10.) Why should intelligent people pay large sums of money to Priests (who are nothing but sinful men), to pray prayers for persons in this condition? The Psalmist says, "In death there is no remembrance of them, in the grave who shall give the thanks?" (Psa. 6:5.)

But I hear someone ask, "Is not there a Hell?" We answer, sure there is. But the Bible Hell is not a place of conscious torment by forged-tail devil or otherwise. The Hell mentioned in the Bible is the condition of death, oblivion, the tomb, the grave, or in other words, it is a condition of non-existence. The only word in the Old Testament translated "Hell" is the Hebrew word "sheol," and it is translated more times as "grave" than it is translated "Hell," and means the same thing in each instance. We give a few examples.

Jacob, weighted down with grief because of the supposed

death of his son Joseph, said, "I will go down to my son Joseph, in sheol (Hell), mourning." (Gen. 37:35.) Later, when requested to send Benjamin to Egypt, he said, "My son Benjamin shall not go down with you to Egypt, for if evil befalls him you will bring down my gray hairs with sorrow to (sheol) hell." (Gen. 43:38.) If Hell means conscious torment in fire, we ask: How long would the gray hairs of Jacob last in such a place? Would God make the gray hairs immortal in order to torment them?

Job was a good and Godly man. After he had suffered the loss of all his earthly possessions; his children killed, his wife became his enemy, his neighbors taunted him because of his suffering, his body putrid with running sores, suffering bodily pain and mental anguish, in this awful condition he prayed that God might send him to Hell. "O that thou wouldst hide me in Hell (sheol) until thy wrath is passed." (Job 14:13.) Does any sane person believe that Job prayed that he might go to a place to be tormented and suffer more agony than he was already suffering? If you were in his position would you ask to go to a place where you would be tormented forever? Job then defines Hell. He says, "If I wait, Hell is my house. I have made my bed in the darkness. Our rest is in the dust." (Job 17:13–16.) If darkness, there could be no fire there. Again, he (Job) said, concerning man, "His sons come to honor and he knoweth it not, they are brought low and he perceiveth it not." (Job 14:21.)

Jehovah, through his prophets, foretold that Jesus would go to Hell, and He did. He went to the same Hell to which the other dead go, and he was dead until the third day, when God raised Him. Referring to Him the Psalmist wrote, "Thou wilt not leave my soul in Hell." (Psa. 16:10.) This text is quoted, with approval, by the apostle Peter, in Acts 2:27. If Hell is a place of conscious torment, eternal in duration, then it would have been impossible for Jesus to have gotten out; whereas the Scriptures conclusively prove that He was raised on the third day.

The New Testament deals with the same "Hell." As we know, the New Testament is translated from the Greek and the Greek word "Hades" means the same as the Hebrew word "sheol." In the revised version of the New Testament, the Greek word "Hades" has been left untranslated. Evidently the translators were ashamed to translate it "Hell" after the meaning of eternal torment had been attached to the word. Our common version renders three different words in the New Testament "Hell," and the people have long been taught by a false bunch of preachers that these words mean eternal torture. In not a single instance, as is well known by every preacher worth the name, and scholar, does the word "Hell," as used in the Scriptures, mean a place of conscious torment. Aside from the Greek word "Hades," there are two other words from which the word "Hell" is translated, as appears in the New Testament; to-wit, Gehenna and Tartarus. We will examine some text on each of these.

Addressing Himself to the people of Capernaum, Jesus said, "And thou Capernaum, which art exalted unto Heaven, shall be thrust down to Hell." (Luke 19:15.) I hope no one

is so foolish as to think of Capernaum, the proud city with
its lands, houses and population, in a place of eternal roast-
ing. The people of Capernaum had been greatly favored
and, figuratively speaking, had been exalted highly in the
standards of the peoples and nations; but because of their
misuse of God's blessings they were told by the Lord Jesus
that they, as a people, should be thrust down to Hades; that
is to say, overthrown, destroyed, go into oblivion, or in other
words, that proud city was to be brought to a condition the
same as though it never existed. It is now a historic fact that
Capernaum is so thoroughly buried in oblivion that not even
the site where it stood is definitely known.

Jesus addressed the people of that time in parables or dark
sayings, hence He used the symbolic language as above stated.
"All these things spake Jesus unto the multitudes in parables,
and without a parable, spake He not unto them." (Math.
13:34.) Again He said, "Thou art Peter (Greek, "Petros," a
rock or stone, one of the living stones, strong minded, of
strong character), and upon this rock (Greek, "Petra," mass of
rock, fundamental rock truth, the great truth that Jesus is the
Christ), I will build My church (composed of faithful followers, like St. Peter), and the gates of Hell (Greek "Hades"),
shall not prevail against it." (Math. 16:18.)

Paraphrased, we would understand these words to mean
that Jesus established the church, which is His body, composed of many members (Col. 1:18; 1 Cor. 12:12), and all the
bitter and relentless persecution which has been the experience of His true followers throughout the Gospel Age, and

which has taken them down into Hell, the grave, the same place where He went, should not prevail to their utter extermination because, in God's due time the church would be brought forth in the first resurrection. (Rev. 20:6.)

Again, Jesus said, "I am He that liveth and was dead. Behold, I am alive forevermore, amen; and have the keys of death and Hell (Hades, the grave)." (Rev. 1:18). The keys mean the power to unlock. Jesus' statement here is that once He was dead, but now He has been raised and is alive forevermore, and has the power to unlock the tomb, the grave, the condition of death, and bring forth the dead in the time of the resurrection.

"The lake of fire and brimstone" is several times mentioned in the book of Revelations, which all Christians admit to be a book of symbols. However, most of them, under the influence of the teachings of selfish and ignorant preachers, think and speak of this particular symbol as a literal statement, and that it gives support to the eternal torment doctrine, notwithstanding the fact that the symbol is clearly defined as meaning the second death. "And death and Hell was cast into the lake of fire. This is the second death," etc. (Rev. 20:14.) It is sometimes spoken of as "A lake of fire, burning with brimstone." (Rev. 19:20.) The element brimstone being mentioned to intensify the symbol of destruction, the second death. Burning brimstone is one of the most deadly elements known. It is destructive to all forms of life. The symbolism of this lake of fire and brimstone is further shown by the fact that the symbolic beast and the symbolic false prophet and death and Hell (Hades), as well as the devil and all his followers are destroyed in it. (Rev. 19:20; 20:10, 14, 15; 21:8.)

Dear friends, I would be more than glad if some of these false teachers or their followers who believe in the "Lake of fire and brimstone doctrine" would tell me who is going to keep the fires burning when the devil and all his followers are destroyed in the above mentioned lake? You know the above cited Scriptures plainly states that the Devil will be destroyed in that lake.

All the preachers worthy of the name know that this doctrine of eternal torment in a lake of fire and brimstone is absolutely false but because of their selfish interest (love of money and undeserved honors) they will not out with the truth.

Brother Parsons, take my advice, as one who loves you. If you will tell the truth and come out for the truth boldly, and live with your people. If you don't do this, very soon you will find yourself backed in the corner by the demands of the people for the truth. If you wait until that condition is reached then the only thing that you could do would be to get out as quickly as you can because the sight of you would become a stench to the moral nostril of truth loving people.

Richard J. Hill

>«

American Red Cross

Immediately following the catastrophe of June 1st of last year, the American Red Cross was called in and given carte blanche authority to handle the problems of relief and reconstruction.

The story of their activities during the following months is too well known to necessitate repetition. In the very first days following the riot immediate relief was necessary to almost all of the victims, regardless of class or resources.

It was then that vast hordes thronged the Booker T. Washington school, where the Red Cross had established their offices, pleading for the barest living necessities in the way of shelter, food and clothes. This first crisis gradually became alleviated, as those people with some resources or means at their disposal became able to meet their own personal problems.

However, a great need continued throughout the summer and into the winter, and it will undoubtedly be months or even years before the conditions will be on an equal basis with the days before the Disaster.

Records on file in the Red Cross office show that during the seven months between June 1st and January 1st, they had handled the cases of 2,480 families (8,624 persons), that nearly one-half million feet of lumber and 50,000 yards of cloth were distributed, and that a total expenditure of $100,000.00 was made for actual relief among the sufferers.

The following schedule, taken from the official report of the Red Cross, will give some conception as to the scope of the work handled:

Total number of families registered: 2,480

Total number of persons in these families: 8,624

Families definitely relieved with clothing, beds, bed clothing, tentage, laundry equipment, cooking utensils, dishes, material for clothes, etc.: 1,941

Churches housed in Red Cross Tents: 8

Prescriptions furnished (outside of Hospital): 230

Medical service (in field given to maternity, typhoid and infant cases): 269

Small property adjustments: 88

Transportation furnished (estimate): 475

Telegrams sent or received (relatives to riot victims): 1,350

The American Red Cross officially closed its Disaster relief work on December 31, 1921, leaving as a legacy to the colored people the Maurice Willows Hospital, at 324 North Hartford Street. This hospital, as it now stands, is the culmination of the medical relief work done during more troublous times. A great deal of care has been exercised in bringing this institution up to date and making it thoroughly modern, and this hospital probably stands as the most constructive piece of work done by the Red Cross here in Tulsa. Appreciation of it will best be shown by its future, since it is being turned over to the colored race for their operation and management.

>«<

Some of the Activities of
A. J. Smitherman, in Tulsa, Oklahoma

Edited and published the *Tulsa Star*, a weekly newspaper founded by him in Muskogee, where it was published as the *Muskogee Star*. Moved to Tulsa in the spring of 1913. For three years edited and published the *Daily Tulsa Star*.

Was a conscientious Democrat and because of his influence with men did do much good for his race in a political way. It was largely through his influence that the colored people of Tulsa enjoyed absolute freedom in the exercise of franchise. He was uncompromising and persistent in the conscientious fight he waged with tongue and pen for equal rights for his people. He hated Jim Crowism and its kindred evils with all his soul and fought it at all times because as he said: "It is wrong in principle and can not bring good results."

He contended successfully for a precinct election board composed entirely of colored men when his effort to get colored men placed on such boards with white men had failed. It was necessary to redistrict the city, but this was done, and Tulsa had the distinction of being the first and only city in the country having an election board composed exclusively of colored men. Mr. Smitherman himself served on this board the first year as Inspector of Elections. The

board was composed of representatives of both dominant
political parties, as required by law, and the members served
the city, county and state with much credit to themselves and
their race.

This and many other things that came to pass in Tulsa,
under a Democratic city administration, as well as county
and state governments of the same political colors, tended
to justify and strengthen the editor of the *Tulsa Star* in his
position for democracy, and many erstwhile, hide-bound
Republicans, by reason of racial traditions, became identified with the Democratic party. This board, a colored hospital and a public library for colored people, maintained by a
Democratic city administration, were all abolished under a
succeeding Republican city administration.

In 1917, when a mob burned the homes of twenty colored
families in Dewey, Oklahoma, A. J. Smitherman went in
person to the mob-ridden town and investigated the trouble
and voluntarily reported his findings to Gov. R. L. Williams,
which resulted in the arrest of 36 men, including the mayor
of the town.

In 1918, when an attempt was being made to lynch a
young colored man by a mob at Bristow, Oklahoma, A. J.
Smitherman, who was then serving the county of Tulsa as
Justice of the Peace, took three willing colored men and
hastened to the scene, after sending urgent telegrams to the
Governor asking for state aid. The young man was saved but
Smitherman was betrayed to the mob by a colored man who
still lives in Bristow. After more than an hour in the hands

of the mob he escaped and fearlessly published the facts in his paper.

A little later in 1918, editor Smitherman attracted considerable publicity when he and his brother, J. H. Smitherman, went to the home of a prominent white man, head of a large public corporation and secretary of the District Exemption Board, and forcibly took away an aged colored woman who had been brought by the family from Louisiana and was being held in peonage. He took the woman to his own home and kept her there as his guest until relatives came for her. For this act he was haled before the County Council of Defense and tried on a charge of being "dangerous to the peace and security of our country." He was denied counsel but bravely stood his ground and defended himself when he saw they intended to confiscate his plant. One of the members of the Council of Defense who was friendly to the editor said afterwards, "Only Smitherman's nerve and manliness saved him."

In 1919, when President Wilson was touring the country espousing his League of Nations program, editor Smitherman was one of the few selected by the Governor to serve on a committee to receive the President, and was one of those scheduled for a speech on the occasion of the intended visit of the chief executive of the nation to Oklahoma City. He was the only colored man thus honored.

Colored people of Oklahoma, and many white people, will long remember A. J. Smitherman for the good he has done here. In 1914 when the colored people of Tulsa awoke one morning to find themselves viciously and wantonly assailed by a pastor of one of Tulsa's leading white churches and consulted among themselves, Smitherman nobly came to the defense of his people in a very able article which appeared in the *Tulsa World* in answer to the attack of the white preacher, which has been heralded not only from his pulpit but in the columns of the *Tulsa World*.

His retort was so timely, so ably written and answered the absurd charges of the white preacher against the colored race as a whole, that even white men and women commended it. The editor received many letters of commendation and tokens of appreciation from leading people of both races. He also received invitations to speak in white churches following the publication of his article.

It is said the pastor tried to form a "committee" (a mob) to wait on Smitherman because of the article, but in this he failed.

The *Tulsa Star* was a recognized power in the politics of Oklahoma because of its wide circulation and influence. Its plant, valued at $40,000 or more, was one of the best equipped printing plants owned by members of the race in the country, employing both white and colored workmen. This plant, as well as the editor's home, was completely destroyed in the massacre of June 1, 1921, and the editor forced into exile with his wife and five children following absurd charges growing out of the riot the night before. It has been charged that his paper was responsible for the "uprising of colored people against the white people of Tulsa" and that he organized the colored men in his office to resist the mob in its attempt to lynch Dick Roland.

>«

Mob Fury and Race Hatred as a National Danger
(Extracts from Literary Digest, *June 18, 1921)*

"There is one problem in American life for which I foresee no solution. It is the race problem, the Negro question." These words of Grover Cleveland are recalled by the *Louisville Courier-Journal* in its editorial discussion of the sudden and appalling flare-up of mob fury and race hatred in Tulsa. In this Oklahoma city, which according to one of the journals "has the highest per capita wealth of any city in the world," the rumor that a colored boy was to be lynched brought a crowd of armed Negroes to the jail to prevent it. With the white mob and black confronting one another, somebody fired a shot, and the result was a pitched battle with scores of casualties, the burning of the city's Negro section, and the addition, as the *New York Evening Post* remarks, of "a ghastly chapter to the record of a national disgrace." For while the immediate cause of the Tulsa tragedy has been concisely described as "an impudent Negro, an hysterical girl, and a yellow-journal reporter," the conditions which provided the tinder for this spark are not peculiar to Tulsa or Oklahoma but exist in varying degree, we are told, in all parts of the country where the Negro is numerous enough to be a problem. According to the editor of a New York Negro weekly, race war lies latent in many American cities, and "as for New York City, it is a magazine. All it needs is to have a fuse touched off." The causes behind the Tulsa explosion and similar outbreaks of the last few years, editorial observers tell us, are: the lynch-law spirit, peonage, race prejudice, economic rivalry between blacks and whites, radical propaganda, unemployment, corrupt politics, and the new Negro spirit of self-assertion. Among the remedies proposed are: new legislation, strict and impartial law enforcement, unionization of the Negroes, and the Golden Rule.

"The Tulsa horror" moves the *Kansas City Journal* to reflect upon "the narrowness of the margin which separates civilization from savagery." "We have in this country an ugly race problem, and to ignore it is only to postpone the reckoning," declares the *St. Louis Post-Dispatch*, which has not forgotten the race war of four years ago in its neighbor city, East St. Louis, in which 125 persons were killed. This problem, the *Post-Dispatch* assures us, "can not be solved by riot, by burnings and killings." "We are headed in this country toward a race conflict greater than the confines of a city—greater, perhaps, than a state," declares the *Star* of the same city, which asks: "Are we going to keep on going in the direction in which we are headed?" "No community knows when it may be marred by similar outrages," says the *Oklahoma City Times*, which is convinced that "the danger of the racial disturbances is increased by the orgy of terrorism in Tulsa." "It is not an issue in which is involved the one true conception of government itself," avers the *Tulsa World*. "Mob violence has become common, and if the tendency is not checked, one may not measure the depths of sorrow to come," says the Oklahoma City, Oklahoma, *Leader*. "If the Tulsa collision had occurred at Vera Cruz the American people would have deplored the lawlessness of the Mexicans and found it shocking," remarks the *New York Times*, and the *Nashville Tennesseean* thinks that "the crime of Tulsa will make many of us hesitate before we condemn other races as being unqualified for self-government." "This is not the first race riot within recent years to occur outside of the Mason-Dixon line," notes the *Wilmington Every Evening*, which recalls the following facts:

"In East St. Louis, Ill., which is distinctly a Northern city, 125 persons were killed on July 7, 1917. In Washington, D.C., seven persons were killed and scores injured in the riots which began July 19, 1919. A few days later, beginning July 26, in Chicago, which is certainly not a Southern city, 38 persons were killed and 500 wounded. On October 2, the same year, in Elaine, Ark., which calls itself Midwestern, 30 persons were killed and hundreds were wounded in the street-fighting. Three days before that, in Omaha, Neb., which is certainly Western, three persons were killed in race riots and many wounded. The mayor of the city was hanged by rioters, but cut down in time to save his life."

The guilt of the Tulsa tragedy, avers an outspoken Southern paper, the *Dallas News*, "attaches itself mostly to the white race," and in the *Emporia Gazette* we read: "Of course it was not the best of the white race that created the

hellish situation in Tulsa. But none the less, the best of the
white race is responsible. The leadership of a community is
responsible for the deeds of the community."

"No matter who kills the most, mobs are an indictment of
all citizens, and of the best citizens more than any of the others," agrees the *Call*, a Negro paper published in Kansas City;
and it adds "we maintain that it is white civilization that is
on trial when Negroes are persecuted, for it is the law as
created by the Anglo-Saxon which is treated with contempt
when our rights are overridden." "We are wondering where is
an Uncle Sam that will hear the cries of the innocent women
and children at Tulsa," exclaims another Negro paper, the
St. Louis Argus; and in still another, the *Black Dispatch*, of
Oklahoma City, we read: "Whatever the issue, the fact remains undisputed that in Tulsa, in a white-man's country, the
Negroes were attempting to uphold the law and white men
were attempting to destroy it."

The nation must awake to what lynch law and race riots
are costing it, our press earnestly admonish us. This Tulsa
horror will be featured in scare-heads in every newspaper
in Mexico City, and will make it still harder for our state
department to convince the Mexicans that we are in deadly
earnest about the protection of American life and property,
remarks the *Chicago Evening Post*, which goes on to say: "At
this moment we are withholding valuable aid to the Mexican
government because we doubt the safety of American life
and property under its jurisdiction, but in Mexican eyes the
Tulsa explosion will knock the high horse out from under

us." Moreover, it adds, such outbreaks "damage the United States more than we realize in the eyes of foreign nations." "Americans have been loud in the denunciation of the pogroms in Poland, of the massacres in Armenia and Russia and Mexico, and they were ready to go to war to avenge the victims of the barbarous German war-lords, but unless we can create a public sentiment in this country strong enough to restrain such intolerant outbreaks as Tulsa has just witnessed, we shall be unable in the future to protest with any moral weight against anything that may happen in less-favored parts of the world," remarks the *Houston Post*, which warns us that "the race problem is not being solved in any part of the country."

Tulsa's outburst of race warfare "was as unjustifiable as it was unnecessary," remarks the *Tulsa World*. The events which made up this tragedy of errors are outlined by Walter F. White in a Tulsa dispatch to the *New York Evening Post*:

"The immediate cause of the riot was a white girl who claimed that Dick Rowland, a colored youth of nineteen, attempted to assault her. Sarah Page, the girl, operated an elevator in the Drexel Building in Tulsa. She said the colored boy had seized her arm as she admitted him to the car. Rowland declares that he stumbled and accidentally stepped on the girl's foot. She screamed. Rowland ran. The following day the *Tulsa Tribune* told of the charge and arrest of Rowland.

"Chief of Police John A. Gustafson, Sheriff McCullough, Mayor T. D. Evans, and a number of reputable citizens, among them a prominent oil operator, all declared that the girl had not been molested; that no attempt at criminal assault had been made. Victor F. Barnett, managing editor of the *Tribune*, stated that his paper had since learned that the original story that the girl's face was scratched and her clothes torn was untrue.

"Soon after the *Tribune* appeared on the streets on Tuesday afternoon there was talk of a lynching mob" to avenge the purity of a white woman. Rowland was then removed to the county jail, located on the top floor of the Tulsa County court house, a substantial building of three stories. Sheriff McCullough stated to me that as early as four o'clock on Tuesday afternoon (the *Tribune* reached the streets with the story of the alleged assault at 3:15 p.m.) Commissioner of Police J. M. Adkison informed him that there was talk of lynching Rowland that night.

By nine o'clock there were from 300 to 400 whites around the court house. About 9:30 twenty-five Negroes came up to the court house armed to protect Rowland. The sheriff persuaded them to go home, but in an hour they returned, their number increased to seventy-five. The sheriff again persuaded them to go home, when a shot was fired. Then in the sheriff's own words, "all hell broke loose."

"Armed mobs of whites broke into hardware stores and pawnshops and looted them, taking weapons and ammunition. Colored men fought gamely, one of them accounting for five members of a mob that attacked the colored section. Near daybreak a pitched battle was in progress with the 'Frisco tracks as a dividing line between the two forces. Shortly afterward the white mobs, numbering by then more than 10,000, invaded the Negro section, the colored men resisting determinedly. Cans of oil were secured and fires started. Firemen attempting to quench the first of these flames were fired upon and withdrew."

The *Tulsa Tribune* and *World* agree the trouble could have been nipped in the bud by decisive action on the part of the city authorities in dispersing the mob as soon as it began to form, and correspondents represent Gov. J. B. A. Robertson as sharing this view. "Undoubtedly the trouble could have been arrested in its incipiency had prompt and intelligent action been taken by officials," declares the *Muskogee Phoenix*, and the *Times-Democrat* of the same Oklahoma city agrees that "in Tulsa the law-enforcement branches were absolutely paralyzed in face of the riots for twenty-four hours." "The accumulation of all the stories relating to the disaster clearly indicates that this is the culmination of a protracted disrespect for law in this city through a long period of time," affirms the *Tulsa Tribune*.

But behind the immediate factors in the Tulsa outbreak editorial observers search for deeper causes. "One incident never causes a race riot; the causes accumulate for weeks and months before the outbreak," remarks James Weldon Johnson, secretary of the National Association for the Advancement of Colored People, who goes on to say: "If the stories told by refugees from Oklahoma are true, conditions virtually of slavery, similar to those laid bare recently by

Governor Dorsey in Georgia, prevail in Oklahoma. Robbery of Negro tenants, brutalities of every description, burning of homes, and enforced labor for a mere subsistence wage will inevitably bring about trouble."

So long as the Negro is denied in whole or in part the rights and immunities guaranteed him under the white-man's law, "the way is open to the repetition of such tragedies as that which happened in Tulsa," avers the *New York World*, in which we read further:

"Government ceased for the time being to exist and the streets of Tulsa ran with blood. But in vast sections of the country government has a habit of ceasing to exist where the legal rights of the Negro are concerned. Although white men are sometimes lynched when accused of crime the general presumption is that they will not be. Although black men are often not lynched when accused of crime, the general presumption in many parts of the United States is that they are likely to be. Out of that presumption came Tulsa's race war."

"The core of the situation is the existence of a latent spirit of lynching," thinks the *New York Evening Post*. Of a changing attitude on the part of the Negro, the *New York Globe* says:

"Because of his experiences as a soldier and on account of the higher value placed upon his labor during the war period he has become less submissive. Whether for good or for evil it is a fact that when attacked by white men he is more likely to shoot back than he was five years ago."

The Socialist *New York Call*, after interviewing Mr. Chandler Owen, editor of the *Messenger*, on the Tulsa riot, reports that "A potent cause," Mr. Owen believes, "is the recent wave of unemployment, which has hit white workers much harder than colored workers, for the simple reason that the Negroes work for lower wages, and are therefore the last to be discharged. This has caused a great deal of resentment among the white workers, who accuse the Negroes of taking away their jobs."

The *Indianapolis News* thinks that there is much in the argument of the *Chicago Tribune* that corrupt politics is the real villain in the Tulsa tragedy and in other American race riots. Says the *Chicago Tribune*:

"If in Tulsa, Chicago, Springfield, or East St. Louis, it were not for the profitable alliance of politics and vice or professional crime, the tiny spark which is the beginning of all these outrages would be promptly extinguished. We should have peace in our communities and the race issue would never reach the point of madness.

"Corrupt politics is directly responsible for race riots. Let us face that fact and not lose ourselves in secondary considerations. Race riots are not problems of race; they are problems of government. There will be no race riots where politics has not corrupted government."

>«

A Law Firm

The colored law firm of Spears, Franklin & Chappelle, with commodious offices now at 107 ½ North Greenwood Avenue, of this city, was formed on the second day of June, 1921, and temporary quarters opened up in a tent at 607 East Archer Street. The formation of this law partnership grew out of the then present situation. The great holocaust of June 1, 1921, had left the colored section in ashes and in ruins. Where imposing business buildings and stately mansions had stood just a few days before were now nothing but heaps of ruins and charred things burned beyond recognition. The people were in confusion and, in many instances, utter helplessness. These brilliant young minds were not long in seeing that if the morale of the race in these parts was to be preserved and their property conserved something must be done at once. After a hasty formation of the partnership the temporary office-tent was erected and fitted up with typewriters and other necessary things—shingle was hung out and the people invited to make the "office" their headquarters. It was in this "office" that more than four million dollars in claims against the city of Tulsa and various insurance companies were prepared. It was in this office that thousands of people came daily for consultation, consolation and advice as to what was best to do. One member of the firm was busy mailing out "call" for help for the riot victims. These calls went out by the thousands to every great Negro organization in the United States and it took a long time to complete the work. This pioneer "office" furnished help and stationery, except in a very small way, free of charge to the Relief Board that had been organized.

It was not until late in the month of November, 1921, that the firm was able to dismantle its "office" and move to a sure enough office on the second story of the Howard Building, 107 ½ North Greenwood, as above referred to. And during the long hot days, and cold days too as a matter of fact, this firm worked away in their effort to safeguard the interests of the people. The work was so big—the task so stupendous—that the boys found it absolutely necessary to work many Sundays. Through it all, there was one thing particularly noticeable and that was the "smile" on their faces and the happy laugh so often indulged in by them. They made it a rule to allow no one to come in their "office" or around them with sad faces. This was no easy task. With want and famine and dire distress stalking all about and women and little children in rags and utter poverty on every hand, it took cool nerves and limitless faith in God to do this. Amid such squalor and barren waste and wreck and ruin on every hand every laugh heard appeared to be a mockery and every smile hypocrisy.

It was on the thirteenth day of August, 1921, that this firm of lawyers, the first to do so, filed suit in the district court to enjoin and restrain the city dads from interfering or in any way molesting the colored people in the rebuilding of their homes that had been licked up in the flames of June 1, 1921. It will be remembered that the city commissioners had, on the seventh day of June, 1921, passed and promulgated a fire ordinance that had for its obvious purpose the making of it an impossibility for the people of color to rebuild their homes.

A signal victory was won by this firm of lawyers in this suit and this thing did more than any other one thing to nerve the race for the work that lay before it. Every Negro that was arrested for the violation of any of the older fire ordinances this firm, without charge, defended him and in every case succeeded in getting him out of the trouble thus brought on in his effort to prepare shelter for his family and himself. The firm is yet undaunted and is now preparing to bring suits against the city for clients for the loss of property sustained in the fire of June 1, 1921. Without any outside financial help and without any loud talking or empty promises, this splendid firm of lawyers are doing their duty just as often as the days come, in the matter of taking care of their clients and their race generally in this neck of the woods.

>«

The Jackson Undertaking Co.

This is an establishment which is a credit to any city; in fact, it is hard to equal and unexcelled in cities of many times the population of Tulsa. Mr. S. M. Jackson, the general manager and senior member of the firm, and his partner, Mr. J. H. Goodwin, through their splendid service and kind and courteous treatment of the public, have worked up a business that is a monument to Negro business and efficiency.

Before the disaster this firm was one of the best equipped establishments in the Southwest, carrying a line of caskets in value from the cheaper grades to the thousand dollar styles of couches, etc., with hearses and cars to correspond. Their latest addition was a ten thousand dollar family car.

In a day all of this was swept away leaving only the hearse and family car (through the kindness of some friends who drove these out of danger).

Mr. Jackson is a graduate of Alcorn A. & M. College, Alcorn, Miss. He is also a graduated and specialized embalmer, having completed this course at a Cincinnati school of embalming. He, therefore, understands all the arts of his profession and this is one of the reasons for his splendid success.

These successful business men have invested heavily in real estate, Mr. Goodwin owning and controlling some of Tulsa's most valued property in our sections. He was one of the heavy losers along this line when the fire of June 1 swept away years of accumulation.

>«<

Messrs. Henry and J. H. Nails are two of Tulsa's leading business men. Before the disaster they owned a modern Shoe Shop equipped with all machinery needed to conduct a high class shop. Their loss was estimated at over $4,000. Since the disaster they have re-opened in their quarters at 121 N. Greenwood, and in addition to having a well equipped shop they carry a full line of Black Swan records.

>«<

Second View of City of Ruins

St. Louis Argus, APRIL 21, 1922

GEORGE W. BUCKNER, SPECIAL REPRESENTATIVE

OF THE NATIONAL URBAN LEAGUE

TULSA—"Wonderful" is the spontaneous acclaim of anyone who visits Tulsa today after seeing the burned area immediately following the disaster there June 1st of last year. The former business section which consisted largely of Greenwood Avenue has been transformed from ragged, unsightly walls to modern structures where small, thriving businesses of every kind are meeting the needs of the people. The formed residential sections which resembled a camp of soldiers in war, having been covered with tents and improvised shacks, are now being rapidly replaced by more substantial homes. But very few of the tents furnished by the Red Cross now remain. So much for a hasty material perspective.

What about the spirit now manifested by the Negroes? Let it be said unreservedly that the spirit exhibited from the beginning by the Tulsa Negroes, on the whole, should be the pride of the whole race. Under the most cruel and soul-crushing conditions they have simply put their backs against the wall determined to die, if needs be, in Tulsa.

One well-to-do man epitomized the general feeling when he said, "I told one of the commissioners the other day when he asked me what I was going to do, that I was going to start over right here in Tulsa where I started before." Most of the people who had acquired any property at all had secured

THE NATION MUST AWAKE

it there. It is but natural, therefore, that they felt bound to their home. With this feeling the Negroes have succeeded in squelching the agitation about taking their land for industrial purposes. They have succeeded in preventing the fire zone from being extended, and in winning to their cause many of the prominent white people. Other problems which appear insolvable by Tulsa Negroes alone, however, are observed, and these strike to the very roots of their future progress.

PRESENT ECONOMIC STATUS

In the first place, the wealth of the Negro of Tulsa has been grossly exaggerated. Much of the property which was controlled by Negroes was heavily mortgaged. Several Negroes each, however, owned from ten to twenty houses with a rental income ranging between $150 and $350 per month. These, for the most part, were of the small three-room type. There was also one block of excellent homes ranging in values between $3,000 and $5,000 each owned largely by professional people. Most of this property was entirely wiped out. The majority of the business section has always been either heavily mortgaged or owned by whites. What the Negroes would have accomplished in another three years can only be estimated.

The new buildings now being erected by Negroes are going up "on paper." The interest rates are exorbitant and carpenters and bricklayers are charging $12.00 per day for their labor. There is not a new building put up by Negroes that is completed because the borrowed sum in each case has given out. Authentic sources, white and black, assert that the

people simply will be forced to figure closely to meet their
notes. Indeed, the next twelve months will be the real test of
the economic strength of the Tulsa Negro. It is commend-
able, however, that the credit of many of the Negroes has
already been re-established, for several homes and businesses
have even been built on "open account."

LARGE SUMS NOT PROVIDED

The public should also know that the large sums which certain
national Negro organizations promised to give were nothing
more, apparently, than skillfully calculated propaganda for
additional members. Too much cannot be said, however, in
praise of the National Association for the Advancement of
Colored People which gathered and expended more than
$3,500 in relief and legal work. In this connection, mention
should also be made of the constructive piece of social service
work done by the Red Cross which secured and expended
upwards of $100,000 in relief work. The mere pittance doled
out by two Negro organizations to their individual members
was indeed a shameful reproach upon intelligent leadership.
The lump sums, however small, should have been used con-
structively, for instance, toward the building of houses, office
buildings, or the establishment of businesses. Tulsa seriously
needs houses and business establishments and those that are
in process of construction must be adequately financed. The
"Brotherhood of Man" is indeed meaningless unless these
people, on a purely business basis, are tided over this, their
most critical period.

Furthermore, the great majority of the former home own-
ers can now get no credit at all, not even at the excessive rates.
The ultimate result will be turning over of their land to the
white people. These people, as you see, will have experienced
both a "burning out" and a "freezing out." Because of the
mild winter there has fortunately been no acute suffering or
need of extra food and clothing. Thus the economic situation
in Tulsa must be viewed now by the country at large, not in
the light of sentiment, but upon sound business principles.
Economic rehabilitation will mean the rebirth of Tulsa's
Negro population and economic failure will mean death to
the spirit of a deserving people, and shame to the whole race.

LACK OF SOCIAL LEADERSHIP

In addition to the economic problems which these Negroes
face, is another of equal importance—the lack of social leadership. Perhaps it is safe to say that there is no city in our
country today which offers a greater opportunity for social
service than Tulsa. Here eight or ten thousand Negroes live
in an entirely segregated section. Their contact with the
whites outside of business and domestic relations has almost
been nil, and they have seemed not only to be satisfied under
such conditions, but to have capitalized on their isolation,
using it as the stimulus to race pride and race elevation. The
needs and accomplishments of the Tulsa Negro have not,
therefore, been made known to the whites. In this connec-
tion it should be stated that much good was accomplished by
the Colored Y.M.C.A. before it became inactive in the late

summer following the disaster. This work was supported by the colored people as only a few of the influential whites had become acquainted with the more intelligent Negroes.

In an effort to develop a social service program which would effectuate co-operative relations between the races, the National Urban League dispatched me to Tulsa a few days after the riot and again in July. I am now writing en route from Tulsa, after a two weeks' stay there where again I have been in touch with the leaders among both white and colored groups, for the purpose of establishing a branch of the Urban League Movement. I found that the leaders among the Negroes now realize that there must be in Tulsa a social service agency with strong leadership to develop the proper influence among the men and women and to build a better and more stable citizenship. This feeling has been strengthened by the fact that the lawless elements which formerly found Tulsa a convenient market to ply their trades are fast disappearing and their places are rapidly being taken by stable Negro families, coming largely from Texas.

Fortunately, there are many whites who also sense the situation among Negroes with intelligence and sympathy. They not only are imbued with sentiment, but are also filled with the desire to improve the lot of all who dwell in Tulsa. Here could be mentioned the names of several ministers, business men, lawyers, club women and others—all prominent and intensely interested in better conditions among Negroes.

It now appears that an Urban League will be established in Tulsa within a short time and these leaders, black and white, working together must provide some group recreational facilities for Negroes; must handle their industrial opportunities more intelligently; must see that the school plants now little used offer evening classes for the working girls and women and for the men who are employed in industrial and household occupations; must prevail upon the church to socialize its program and to insist upon a better trained Negro ministry; must remove ignorant Negro political leaders who are the prey of white ward heelers, both of whom are enemies of good citizenship; must see that justice in every respect is meted out alike to all citizens, irrespective of color. In brief, such a movement must strive in the name of Christian statesmanship to help these people of remarkable hope in the face of adversity to become citizens in every sense of the word and to share equality with other racial groups all the joys as well as the sorrows of the city, thus uplifting the whole community life of Tulsa.

>«

Mme. Geo. W. Hunt, proprietress of the Creole Beauty Parlor, is originally of Louisiana. She came to Tulsa from Beaumont, Texas, in 1911, where she was manager of a branch office established by Vanderhoof Co., of South Bend, Indiana. She resigned this position with great honor and much regret by the company and her many patrons.

Mme. Hunt is a very successful, industrial and energetic business woman. Her amiable and amicable qualities make her a perfect success. She is the only Colored Hair Dresser in this city that uses distilled water for shampooing. Must say that she is top-notch and capable of handling both White and Colored trade.

This progressive lady is a widow, and has a daughter, Thelma, who resides in Los Angeles, California. Thelma will graduate next year from High School at the tender age of 15 years.

Mme. Hunt owns a beautiful lot in Gary, Ind., and four lots in New Jersey, which she holds deeds for. During the disaster she was one of the lucky ones who did not get burned out. She was well cared for all through the trouble by her many White friends of her Church, which is the Holy Family Catholic Church.

Such women as Mme. Hunt are indeed a credit to the community in which they live.

In writing Mme. Geo. W. Hunt, address all mail to Tulsa, Oklahoma.

Partial List of Losses
Sustained by Victims of the Tulsa Riots

PARTIAL LIST OF LOSSES

Sustained by Victims of the Tulsa Riots

PROPERTY OWNERS	LOSSES
Mr. Jim Cherry	$ 50,000
Mr. O. Gurley	65,000
J. H. Goodwin	30,000
Mr. John Gist	25,000
Dr. R. T. Bridgewater	32,000
Mrs. Lula T. Williams	85,000
Mrs. Annie Partee	35,000
Mrs. Jennie Wilson	25,000
Mr. A. Brown	15,000
Mr. J. B. Stradford	125,000
Mr. A. L. Phillips	40,000
Mr. W. H. Smith (Welcome Grocery)	40,000
Elliott & Hooker, Clothiers and Dry Goods	45,000
Dr. A. F. Bryant	30,000
Mr. C. W. Henry	25,000
Jackson Undertaking Co.	15,000
Mr. T. R. Gentry	25,000
Prof. J. W. Hughes	15,000
Mr. S. M. Jackson	15,000

NORTH GREENWOOD STREET.

RESIDENCE	SIZE	BUSINESS	VALUE
2-Story Brick			$ 15,000
101—Woods'	70x80	Earl Real Estate Co.	
103		Bayers & Anderson, Tailors.	
103½		R. T. Bridgewater, Physician.	
103½		T. R. Gentry, Real Estate.	
102½		Wesley Jones, Physician	
103½		James M. Key, Physician.	
103½		Mrs. Mary E. J. Parrish, School.	
103½		Two Apartments.	
103½		Oklahoma Sun Office, Theo. Baughman.	
WILLIAMS' BLDG.	25x35		$ 12,500
3-Story Brick.			
102		Dr. J. J. McKeever.	
102		Mrs. Lulu Williams, Confectionery.	
102—Second Floor		Apartments.	
102—Third Floor		Offices.	
MRS. E. G. HOWARD'S BLDG.			
	25x80		$ 8,000
2-Story Brick.			
107		Barber Shop.	
107½		Safety First Loan Co.	
107½		Mrs. Sarah Whitaker, Rooms.	
BRYANT BLDG.	50x90		$ 15,000
2-Story Brick.			
108		Bryant's Drug Store, Dr. A. F. Bryant.	
108½		Rooming House.	
110		C. L. Netherland, Barber Shop.	
PHILLIPS	25x80		$ 15,000
2-Story Brick.			
111		Hardy & Hardy, Restaurant.	
111½		Hardy & Hardy, Rooms.	
GURLEY BLDG.	50x140 80 Rooms		$ 55,000
2-Story Brick.			
112		Brunswick Billiard Parlor.	
112½		Gurley Hotel.	
114		Dock Eastman & Hughes, Cafe.	
PHILIP'S BLDG.	50x80		$ 12,500
2-Story Brick.			
115		Carter's Barber Shop.	
115½		E. A. Hardy, Furnished Rooms.	

```
117  ...................  ...............  Gentry, Neely & Vadel, Billiards.
117  ...................  ...............  Oquawka Cigar Store.
GURLEY BLDG.  O. W. Gurley.
          ..................25x60.............................................$ 10,000
     2-Story Brick.
119  ...................  ...............  A. S. Newkirk, Photographer.
119½ ...................  ...............  S. G. Smith, Insurance.
119½ ...................  ...............  Bashears & Franklin, Attorneys and Oil
                                             Deal.
119½ ...................  ...............  Smith's Apartment.
DIXIE BLDG.  Redfern 50x130...........................................$ 50,000
     1-Story Brick.
120  ...................  ...............  Dixie Theater.
120½ ...................  ...............  Samuel Stokenberry, Shoe Shiner.
120  ...................  ...............  J. R. Bell.
GIST BLDG.  Gist......25x80.............................................$ 12,500
     2-Story Brick.
121  ...................  ...............  J. P. Gist, Barber
121  ...................  ...............  Nails Brothers, Shoe Repair Shop.
121½ ...................  ...............  Gist Rooms.
SMITH BLDG. .........50x120..............................................$ 30,000
     2-Story Brick.
122  ...................  ...............  Welcome Grocery.
122½ ...................  ...............  Smith's Apartment.
122½ ...................  ...............  Dr. Wells.
122½ ...................  ...............  Dr. Robinson.
122½ ...................  ...............  Dr. P. Travis.
122½ ...................  ...............  Dr. Smitherman.
122½ ...................  ...............  Attorney E. I. Sadler.
122½ ...................  ...............  Y. M. C. A. Rooms.
124  ...................  ...............  Elliott & Hooker, Clothing and Dry
                                             Goods.
GOODWIN BLDG.  ......25x80..............................................$  7,000
     2-Story Brick.
123  ...................  ...............  Union Grocery, Duncan & Clinton.
123½ ...................  ...............  Rooms.
WILLIAMS' BLDG.,
     No. 2  .........25x140..............................................$ 30,000
     2-Story Brick.
129-133 ................  ...............  Dreamland Theater.
129½ ...................  ...............  A. J. Whitley, Physician.
129¼ ...................  ...............  Alexander Hotel.
MRS. TITUS BLDG......20x30.............................................$  1,500
     1-Story Brick.
127  ...................  ...............  Little Pullman Cafe.
MRS. PARTEE BLDG. ..
     (2) ..............15x40..........
     1-Story Frame.
201  ...................  ...............  Cain's Cafe ....................$  1,500
203  ...................  ...............  Dr. R. T. Motley, Office.
HILL'S BLDG  .........25x70.............................................$  8,000
     2-Story Brick.
126  ...................  ...............  Star Printing Co., A. J. Smitherman.
126½ ...................  ...............  Morgan Rooms.
REDWING BLDG.  .....25x100..............................................$ 30,000
     2-Story Stone.
202  ...................  ...............  Wm. Kyle, Druggist.
204  ...................  ...............  Red Wing Cafe, J. L. White.
206  ...................  ...............  Abbie Funche, Tailor.
206½ ...................  ...............  Red Wing Hotel, Mrs. J. T. Pressley.
208  ...................  ...............  Barber Shop, Abner & Hutton, Prop.
STRADFORD BLDG....50x140.............................................$ 50,000
     2-Story Brick.
301  Stradford Hotel...  ...............  Stradford Hotel.
301  "A" ..............  ...............  A. L. Ferguson, Drugs.
CLEANER & CHERRY
     BLDG.  .....25x80..................................................$  8,000
     2-Story Brick.
501  ...................  ...............  Anderson & Person, Groceries.
501½ ...................  ...............  Knights of Pythias.
501½ ...................  ...............  Odd Fellows Hall.
```

FRANKFORT AVENUE, NORTH.

BUILDING	SIZE	BUSINESS	VALUE
BURNETT'S BLDG......40x80			$ 6,000
1½-Story Brick.			
302		T. J. Wiseman, People's Tailoring Co.	
BAKER'S BLDG........40x80			$ 4,500
2-Story Brick.			
304		W. A Baker, Grocery.	
304½		Apartment.	
MRS. MEEKS' BLDG....25x40			$ 750
1-Story Frame.			
502		W. M Curry, Grocery.	
(3) 1-Story Stones..25x100			$ 5,000
525		Johnson's Plumbing Office.	
527		Bell & Little Cafe.	
529		Cold Drinks and Cream Parlor.	
1-Story Frame 15x30			$ 350

CAMERON, EAST.

Blacksmith's Shop.
Loup's Plumbing Office.

STRADFORD BLDG.
Facing Cameron St. Included in Hotel
Bldg.

Waffle House.

ARCHER, EAST.

BUILDING	SIZE	BUSINESS	VALUE
1-Story Brick		B. A. Wayne, Physician.	
1-Story Frame			$ 2,500
206		Rolly Huff, Confectionery.	
1-Story Brick 18x30			$ 1,200
210		A. J. Douglas, Barber Shop.	
1-Story, 4-Room Stucco.			
216		B. F. Smith, Physician.	
1-Story Frame.			
303		H. A. Guess, Attorney	$ 750
305		Rev. W. H. Twine, Real Estate..	750
307		Charles Allen, Tailor	750
1-Story Frame.			
301		Friedman Bros., Grocery	$ 800
1-Story Frame			
314½		R. J. Clark, Tailor	$ 500
316		J. L Locard, Restaurant	800
316½		Wm. Bunns, Shoe Shine Parlor.	250
1-Story Frame.			
318		Ray Smith, Barber Shop	$ 300
1-Story Frame			
328		Woodard & Tillman,	
		Confectionery	$ 400
328		Grace & Warren, Restaurant	300
402	G.	G. W. Hutchins, Attorney.	
416½		L W. Williams, Restaurant	$ 1,200
418		S. L. Neal, Tailor	1,200
2-Story Frame.			
420		Midway Hotel	$ 4,000
421		Grace Johnson, Restaurant	800
1-Story Frame.			
429		Public Library	$ 750
2-Story Frame.			
501		Mrs. Grace Johnson, Rooms	$ 2,500
2-Story Frame.			
505		D. R. Roland, Rooms	$ 5,000
1-Story Stone.			
514		Steam Laundry, Mrs Pastel	$ 3,500
MRS. PARTEE'S BLDG..25x40			
1-Story Brick.			
516		J. L. Grier, Shoemaker	$ 2,500
516		Mrs. Lula Lacy, Restaurant	800
516½		Rooms	1,000

608 ....W. D. Keley, Lunch Counter....   400
MRS. DORA WELLS' BLDG.
     1-Story Frame.
613 ....Mrs Dora Wells, Garment
                                          Factory ....$ 2,500
     2-Story Stone ......50x120..........
614 ....East End Garage, Mr. Williams.. 8,500
     2-Story Frame.
617 ....R. R. Robinson, Physician........ 1,500
     2-Story Frame.
619 ....Louiza White, Fun. Rooms...... 4,000
MYERS BLDG.
     2-Story Brick.
622 ....Jackson Und. Co , S. M. Jackson.$40,000
622½ ....Mrs. N. O. Smith, Beauty Parlor.
622½ ....Dr. L. N. Neal, Chiropractor.
622½ ....Beauty Parlor.

CINCINNATI STREET, NORTH.

RESIDENCE	SIZE	BUSINESS	VALUE
1-Story Frame.			
6		T. D. Jackson, Barber...........$	700
8		Caver French Dry Cleaners......	700
10		T. B. Carter, Billiards...........	800
12		Mrs. Bertha Brown, Restaurant..$	800
14		F. E. Dickson, Tailor............	1,200
16		Cornelius Hunter, Restaurant....	
18		J. W. York, Meats (White)......	850
2-Story Brick.			
	25x80	.........................$ 8,000	
23		P. S. Thompson, Physician. Drugs.	
23½		Hazel Homan, Rooms.	

NORTH ELGIN.

BUILDING	SIZE	BUSINESS	VALUE
1-Story Stone.			
18		T L. Moseley, Shoemaker........$	550
22		Rev. J. H. Hooker, Photographer.	550
F. R. WILLIAMS' BLDG.			
	25x80	.........................$10,000	
2-Story Brick.			
122		Williams' Confectionery.	
122	"A"	F. R. Williams, Real Estate.	
122	"A"	Apartment	
1-Story Frame		Leon Williams, Confectionery....$	2,500
1-Story, 4-room Frame.			
310		Mrs. G. W. Hunt, Beauty Parlor.	
1-Story, 4-room Frame.			
501		Jewel Fuhiman, Grocery (White).$	2,000
520	10-Room, 2-Story Frame with Store Bldg. in connection.		
MRS LENA CHARLSTON.		Mrs L. Charleston, Grocery......$	5,000

DETROIT STREET.

RESIDENCE	NO. ROOMS	PROPRIETOR	VALUE
Rev. Augustus Hicks.		Rev. A. Hicks.	
2-Story Frame	....	....	....$ 3,000
401		Mr. Armstead Bankhead.	
503—2-Story Frame—Basement		Mrs. M. A. Wright.	
507—1-Story Frame—Basement		R. T Bridgwater, Physician.	
511—1-Story Frame—Basement		T. R. Bridgwater, Physician.....$	2,500
		(Occupied by A. J. Smithermon)	
515—1-Story Frame—Basement		Dr. J. J. McKeever..............	4,500
521—1-Story Frame—Basement		Rev W. H. Woods..............	5,000
523—1-Story Frame—Basement		A. C. Andrew...................	3,000
529—1-Story Frame—Basement		H. M. Magill	4,500
531—1-Story Frame—Basement		E. W. Woods	3,000
537—1-Story Frame—Basement		T. R, Gentry	5,000
541—1-Story Frame—Basement		C. D. Brown	3,500
625—1-Story Frame—Basement		J. W. Hughes	7,000

627—1-Story Frame—Basement ....Singer ....

533—1-Story Frame—Basement ....Stovall 6,000

NORTH ELGIN STREET.

RESIDENCE	NO. ROOMS PROPRIETOR	VALUE
STRADFORD BLDG. No. 2.		
2-Story Brick.	Mr. Stradford	$ 3,000
502—1-Story Frame (Double)	Dr. R. T. Bridgwater	2,000
505—1-Story Frame	Mr. Nelson Smith	1,500
506—1-Story Frame	Mrs Oliva Fasset	1,500
507—	Stradford	800
508—		
509—		
510—1-Story Frame	Thomas Nelson	800
511—	P. W. Rose	1,800
513—	Mrs. Glen Stone	
516—1-Story Frame	C. W. Henry (G. W. Bell)	3,000
516 "A"—2-Story Frame	C. W. Henry	2,500
518—2-Story Frame	C W. Henry (Wm. Grace)	800
520—2-Story Frame	Mrs. Lena Charleston	3,000
521—1-Story Frame	Mrs. Mattie Buchanan	500
522—1-Story Frame	(Nilon Randall) Mrs. Partee	7,000
523—1-Story	Hoser Vaden	1,000
524—1-Story	(James Napier)	800
525—2-Story Frame	John McClelland	1,000
522—rear—2-Story Stone	Mrs. Partee	
527—2-Story Frame	Libbie Jackson	2,000
529—1-Story Frame—basement—6 rms.		
and bath	Dr. P. Travis	4,500
535—I. A. Bell	Mrs. Lynch	3,500
536—W. N. Smart—2-Story Frame	W. N. Smart	4,000
540—Ira Ellis		2,000
542—C. L. Netherland—2-Story Brick, 10 rooms, C. L. Netherland		5,000
544—Dr. C B. Wickham, 1-Story Frame		3,000
609—Hannah Carter		800
613—W. A. Miller		800
903—Wm. Clark		
909—Calvin Johnson	Calvin Johnson	900
911—Mrs. Eliza Martin		

EASTOR STREET, EAST

RESIDENCE	NO ROOMS PROPRIETOR	VALUE
315—J. L. Easley	R. T. Bridgewater	$ 3,000
317—A. A. Floyd	R. T. Bridgewater	3 000
407—John Clark		1,000
408—A. E. Tyous	J. B. Stradford	300
409—Jefferson Johnson		1,000
410—Osborn Mourol		1,000
412—E. Johnson		1,250
415—L. Vauns		1,000
417—Mrs. Sarah Richardson		1,000
419—Mrs. Amanda Thomas		1,200
420—L. W. Thompson—2-story Frame	L. W. Thompson	5,000
422—C. F. Gabe		1,500
424—Alice Dunlap		1,200
501—H T. Wilson, Real Estate		2,000
502—Jimmie Lee		600
503—George Kelley		600
504—Mrs. Raxina Townsend		500
505—Robert Carter		500
507—Mrs. Minnie Johnson		2,000
508—W. B. Rankins		1,200
509—W. M. Lewis		1,000
511—J L. Brown		1,000
513—Curley Dansy		650
515—John Haynes		700
517—Ealy Anderson		250
606—Emma Clay		1,400
608—Mrs. Callie Rogers		300
610—Mrs. Silvia Roberts		1,000

611—Rev. H. T. S. Johnson...   900
619—C. L. Livingston...   900
620—Mrs. Ruby Thaw...
621—L. J. Littles..
709—Oscar McDonald 1,000
712—Mrs. Elizabeth Holmes..   750
713—Ruby Thaw   400
715—Lula Jackson   400
717—Mrs. Hybuna Williams...   400
723—W. D. Wilburn..   500
735—Austin McLane, no such number......................................
811—James Jackson   800
901—Mrs. Mary Jackson.. 1,000

EXETER PLACE

RESIDENCE	NO. ROOMS	PROPRIETOR	VALUE
217—W. H. Sphier			1,000
218—John Frazier			1,000
220—Mrs. Henryetta T. Gentry			1,000
222—Mrs. Agnes Johnson			850
224—Mrs Fannie Right		J. H Goodwin	550
301—			
303—J. O. Foushee		Earl Sneed	3,500
305—A. L. Warren		Mrs. Warren	2,000
307—James Hardeman		Mrs. Warren	2,000
308—Lester Drake			1,500
309—N. W. Hodge		Mrs. Warren	2,000
310—Joseph Cason		Virgil Rowe	1,500
311—J. R. Garrett		Virgil Rowe	1,500
313—Mary Casey			
315—E. B. Duncan		Duncan	2,500
317—Buster Mayhue		Virgil Rowe	4,000
319—Cinda Lee		Jno. Swinger	5,000
321—Thomas Lunsford			4,000
401—M F. Howard			600
403—A. M. Tucker			600
404—W. Friend			1,800
405—R. M. Anderson			1,000
407—Charles Colum			850
409—George Hunt			800
411—Henry Kimble			850
413—W L. Jones			
415—N. E. Butler			
423—Charles Driver (Restaurant)		Charles Driver	350
427—Richard Thomas			1,000
510—Mrs. A. Cox, Residence and Grocery.		Mr. and Mrs B. L. Cox	2,000
512—Arthur Scott			800
514—James Yates			1,500
515—			2,000
516—Abe Yates			
517—J. H. Hodnett, 1-story frame, 6 rms.		Mrs Emma Works	2,000
519—Mrs. Emma Works, 1-story frame, 6 rms.		Mrs. Emma Works	2,500
520—Edward Jones			800
522—C. M. Mathews			1,200
531—J H. Smith			4,500
535—M. C. Allen			1,000
537—C. H. Perkins, 1-story frame, 3 rms.		C. H. Perkins	1,000

BRADY EAST.

RESIDENCE	NO. ROOMS	PROPRIETOR	VALUE
308—Wm Jones			1,500
310—Garfield Dixon			800
311—Emma Dixon			1,200
316—N. S. Jones			5,000
318—Mrs. Margaret Davis			3,000
404—Leon Homer			600
412—J. J. Jones			750
502—Benjamin Blythe—House moved			
510—Albert Vernon—House moved			
515—John Williams			1,200

DAVENPORT EAST.

RESIDENCE	NO. ROOMS PROPRIETOR	VALUE
416—Dr. B. A. Wayne, 1-story frame, 6 rms..Dr. B. A. Wayne		3,000

HASKELL EAST.

RESIDENCE	NO. ROOMS PROPRIETOR	VALUE
401—J. H. Goodwin, 2 story frame, 9 rms..J. H. Goodwin		4,000
407—1-Story Brick, 5 rooms..........J. H. Goodwin		1,500
409—1-Story Brick, 6 rooms..........J. H Goodwin		3,500
—2-Story Frame, 5 rooms..........J. H. Goodwin		3,000
—Garage		500

FRANKFORT AVENUE NORTH.

RESIDENCE	NO. ROOMS PROPRIETOR	VALUE
206—Hanery Van Dyke, 2-story brick.... Brockman Bros.		$ 2,500
210—C. W. Drummond, 5 rooms		1,750
212—J. R. Bell, 4 rooms		1,200
214—Francis Hood, 3 rooms		400
216—Thomas Johnson, 3 rooms		400
220—Rufus Allen, 5 rooms		1,200
221—Edward Richardson, 3 rooms		450
224—Edward Howard, 5 rooms		2,250
301—James Jefferson, 4 rooms		1,500
303—G. D. Aytch, 5 rooms		2,000
304—Samuel Perkins, 4 rooms		1,000
305—Hap Watson		5,000
309—Catherine Jackson		1,250
310—S E. Easley		3,000
311—Al Young	Bridgewater	
314—Floyd Gilkey		3,500
316—F. W. Waddell		1,200
317—Rev. A. W. Brown, 8 rooms....S. M Jackson		2,000
318—Alice Staples, 6 rooms..........S. M Jackson		2,000
319—Elmer Williams		1,500
320—Theodore Baughman ....Bridgewater		1,000
320½—D W. Devrow, 2 houses on lot..Stovall		3,500
321—Wright Jones	Bridgewater	1,000
322—Jessie C. Vann	Mrs. Watson	750
323—C. V. Nunley	Bridgewater	2,500
401—Toby Campbell		500
402—Hixie B. Blackman		750
403—Robert Robertson		1,500
403¼ Victor Visher		1,250
404—A. W Tindall		1,250
405—L. T. Johnson		2,500
406—Willie Connor		1,000
407—John Hampton		1,000
408—Charles Berry	Mrs. Watson	1,000
409—W. H. Hicks		900
410—H J. Green		800
411—Emma Anderson		1,500
412—Swuare Nebles		1,200
415—Mrs. Mary Mitchell, 1-Story Frame.Mrs. Mary Mitchell		1,000
416—Mrs. Aurelia E. Watson		2,000
417—Amy Hawkins		1,500
504—Mrs. Mary Simms		1,000
505—Wm. Dysart		1,000
506—Olive Dupree		700
508—Mrs. Sophia Smith		700
511—Mrs. Bonnie Whipple		700
512—W. M. Henderson		1,500
513—Lon Jenkins		500
514—Mondy Lincoln		850
515—Mrs Emma Swinger		2,500
516—Mrs. Margaret McKeever		1,000
519—O. W. Hawkins		2,000
521—M. K. Randles		850
623—Mrs Ella (Watley) Meeks, 2-story frm..Mrs. Ella Meeks		2,500
634—Staley Webb, 1-story frame.......Staley Webb		3,000

GREENWOOD AVENUE NORTH

RESIDENCE	NO. ROOMS PROPRIETOR	VALUE
305—Dock Eastman		1,200
306—Alvin Graves		2,500
306—"A"—E. W. Vaden		2,500
307—Daniel Black		1,000
308—Rev. J. A Johnson, 2-story frame.	Rev. J. A. Johnson	2,500
309—Harvey Hearst		1,200
310—J. E. Fields		1,500
311—Wm. Cherry		1,000
312—Joseph Saunders		1,500
314—Mack Bergman		1,000
315—Sallie Grayson		1,750
316—C B. Turner		1,750
317—G. L. Gasper		1,500
318—Anderson Parker		1,000
319—M. A. Byars		750
321—W. M Haward		1,000
400—W. M. Bruner		2,000
401—Frank Gaylord		950
402—W. J. Wood, Physician		1,250
403—E T. Waters		950
404—Steward Cooper (Laundry)		850
405—Wm. Clark		900
406—Mrs. Ida Berry		1,000
407—Wm. Young		1,000
408—Mrs. Minnie L. Sanders		1,000
408½—W. H. Cohn, Physician		250
409—Mrs. Fannie White		1,000
411—Mrs. Martha A. Newman		700
412—Henry Johnson		950
413—R. C. Carter		950
414—James King		1,000
415—Bud Thomas		1,750
417—Nathaniel Dorset		3,000
418—Mrs Samuel Mackley, 2-story frm.	Mrs. Samuel Mackley	5,000
421—Mrs. Equella Randle		1,000
502—Mrs. May Thompson		1,000
503—A. C. Jackson		500
504—Love Williams		750
505—A. W Williams		1,250
506—Mrs. Jannie Russell		1,000
507—Mrs. Carrie Barner		
508—Barney Cleaver, 2-story frame	Barney Cleaver	2,000
509—W. M. Luper		2,000
510—J B. Burton		2,000
511—Mrs. Camile Colbert		1,000
512—J. H. Golden		1,000
513—J. B. Beason		1,500
514—M C. Edwards		1,000
515—A. F. Bryant		2,000
516—Mrs. Josie Daniels		1,000
519—James Thomas		850
518—Julius Muckroy		850
520—Mary Ananda		850
604—Rev. J. R McClain		
702—James Cherry	James Cherry	4,000
716—A. L. Phillips, 1-story frame	A. L. Phillips	4,000

HARTFORD AVENUE NORTH.

RESIDENCE	NO. ROOMS PROPRIETOR	VALUE
12—L. F. Guess		300
23—Nelson Talbert		300
101—Frank Taylor		1,000
104—Roy Littles		800
106—Henry Richmond		750
108—Jack Scott		1,200
110—W. P. Carter		3,000
111—John Andres		500

```
112—Eva  Bolden .................................................    500
113—Moot  Dallas ................................................
115—Guss  Mitchell ..............................................
116—Mrs.  Emma  O'Connor.......................................
117—John  Thomas ...............................................
118—Mrs.  Emma  Meacher........................................
120—Wm.  Dodd .................................................
121—J.  L  Anderson.............................................
122—Mrs.  Nina  Dickson.........................................   2,500
124—Mrs.  Emry  Malone..........................................   1,750
301—D.  E.  Green...............................................   3,000
303—Mrs.  Julia  Haynes.........................................   1,000
304—Mrs.  Sarah  Burger.........................................    750
305—Mrs.  Sarah  Gaines.........................................    750
306—Hannibal  Rankins ..........................................    500
307—Odis  Easlick ..............................................    750
309—Orlando  Williams ..........................................   1,800
310—Jesse  Edwards .............................................    500
311—Clifford  Warren ...........................................   1,000
312—Mrs.  Retta  Boon...........................................    750
313—George  McAlister ..........................................    750
```

SCHOOLS.

	VALUE
Dunbar Grade School	20,000

CHURCHES.

	VALUE
Methodist Episcopal	1,000
African Methodist Episcopal	2,500
Colored Methodist Episcopal	2,000
Mt. Zion Baptist	6,500
Paradise Baptist	85,000
Metropolitan Baptist	3,000
Union Baptist	2,000
Seventh Day Advent	1,500

HOSPITALS.

	VALUE
Frissell Memorial	3,500

» AFTERWORD «

Anneliese M. Bruner

The first time the police followed me, I was a fifteen-year-old girl walking to school one morning. Most days I would have been wearing a middy with a sailor collar and cuffs, atop a blue pleated skirt. But that particular day was "free dress," one of the rare opportunities for freedom from the monotony and regimentation of our uniforms, a chance to wear to school whatever outlandish 1970s outfit we chose to express ourselves. Striding up Jackson Street in San Francisco's Pacific Heights neighborhood to what was then the upper school campus of the Katherine Delmar Burke School for Girls—wearing my favorite and only pair of platform shoes and a midsize Afro—I noticed a passing black and white slow down when the police officer who was driving saw me.

At that age I was already wary of the police. I had spent eight years of childhood in East Oakland, where police violence against people in my community was rampant, replete with helicopters in the nighttime sky shining high beams on the neighborhood.

So, walking in San Francisco, those three blocks to school from the bus stop seemed interminable. The police didn't just trail me to see where I was going that morning; they circled each successive block as I walked, coming back around to Jackson Street to follow my progress block by block. They wanted me to know they were there. Their goal was intimidation. I was breathless by the time I slipped through the school door but ready to carry on with my day at the exclusive school for the daughters of San Francisco's first families.

»«

I didn't learn about the Tulsa race massacre of 1921 until I was an adult—and read the book my great-grandmother wrote about it. My father, William Bruner Jr., who was raised in Tulsa for part of his childhood, never mentioned the massacre to me when I was growing up. We had a fractured, divorced household, and too much time and energy were consumed in navigating the logistics of spending time together and managing the dynamics of a blended family. I did not have much time alone with my dad, and it took many years for us to have a relationship that permitted us to talk openly and without friction about the things that matter deeply.

I had been living in Washington, D.C., for about ten years in the early 1990s, when my father presented the book to me on one of my annual visits home to California. He was all hush-hush as he pulled the book out of an old manila envelope, letting me know he was entrusting it to me. He acted like someone sharing a secret. Inscribed to my father from a Jones family member, the little red book was slim and compact. I was mystified by his behavior, and he offered the scantest of explanations. I knew he wanted me to do something, but I wasn't sure exactly what. I was only in my midthirties, but he had started calling me the matriarch of the family, a label that made me uncomfortable. The book was yet another opportunity to explore more about the family and my place in it that neither of us knew how to take.

Back home in D.C. I read the book in one sitting and was overcome with anger and grief for what Tulsa's African American community endured and for the planting of the seeds of individual and family trauma that bloomed later in the lives of people who were dear to me when I was a child—my father and his younger brother, my Uncle Richard, and my grandmother Florence, who features as Mary Jones Parrish's young daughter in the book.

I also learned that Tulsa, however imperfect, was more than a place where people came to make money—it was a space where Black people ran their community with some autonomy and authority. In 1921 it was a nexus of Black wealth, ambition, and pride, teeming with independent, educated people like my great-grandmother, Mary Jones Parrish, and returning World War I veterans like my great-grandfather on the other side of the family, Richard Harrison Bruner. I do not know if he was in Tulsa at the time of the event, but the veterans who gathered to rescue Dick Rowland from lynching represented a fervor to fight against antidemocratic practices at home as vigorously as they had abroad.

The Greenwood community in 1920s Tulsa was the proverbial village that embraced and encouraged its residents, animated by the vitality and industry of the people who lived within its boundaries. Greenwood was the entity that permitted them to dream of achieving the rights, rewards, and responsibilities of full participation in the civic life of their community and country. It was a space for them to realize the individual self-determination and prosperity that embodied the American ideal but also to harness the same cooperative spirit that had buoyed African Americans through enslavement, an incomplete Reconstruction, and the draconian racial practices that followed in the wake of Reconstruction's disruption under such legislation as the Compromise of 1877. This failure sabotaged the progress that should have propelled African Americans and the nation toward full civil rights.

Like other Americans, Black Tulsans served their country during the war, but they could not have imagined that planes would fly over their community and shoot and firebomb the whole of it as if it were enemy territory.

More than anything, the deployment of the machinery of war against civilians showed the willingness of authorities to attack Black Americans with the utmost lethality. There was little daylight between state actors and the vicious mob in their hatred and deadly intent toward Black people. Black lives did not matter to Whites who resented "uppity Negroes," nor to local government, which sought to appropriate the land Black Wall Street occupied to satisfy its appetite for growth.

The elements that contributed to the disaster—the view of Black equality as anathema to the natural social order, official complicity in mob violence, and weaponization of legislation in service to monied interests—still animate the American

landscape we inhabit today. Here was a well-to-do community where people were living up to expectations of the larger
society. Nevertheless, they were attacked and their lives upended on a pretext, set upon by a violent mob eager to destroy or seize by force the trappings of a community's success.
Homes were looted and burned, and White people laughed
openly at the newly created unfortunates. Professionals and
laborers alike were left destitute and without recourse, as all
they had worked for was stripped from them. Dignified men
had to flee without even a hat on their heads.

We know that Tulsa's police department deputized White
men to control, and even destroy, Black lives and livelihoods,
as the community defended itself against lynching and
property theft and destruction. The ease of such a decision
is recognizable in today's casual criminalization of Black
Americans. Random activities can turn into a deadly confrontation with law enforcement. The freedom that is promised to all Americans is conditional for Black Americans,
driven by arbitrary measures of whether they are intelligent
enough, industrious enough, humble enough, nonthreatening enough, innocent enough, patriotic enough, and so on.

But in an enlightened society people who are free are not
required to prove they are worthy. Fundamentally, no human
has the authority to grant humanity or worth to another. That
quality stems directly from our existence, and any system that
assumes that authority is simply not credible. Nevertheless,
fear caused by the abuse of power at the institutional level
can cause Black people to try to prove they are respectable

and deserving enough, spinning their wheels in the unten-
able, unwinnable game of approval seeking in a system that
has not evolved past abusing them as it maintains the powerful myth of righteousness. Paradoxically, by internalizing the
measure of worth imposed by a skewed system, those being
unfairly judged often strengthen the pernicious fiction that
one group is authorized to decide the humanity of another.

American history provides abundant examples of others
taking it on themselves to define or proscribe Black life and
humanity and to dole out abuse accordingly. Earlier this year,
a White mob violently attacked the U.S. Capitol in an effort
to overturn the certification of votes for the rightfully elected
president of the United States—after record numbers of
African Americans exercised their political power. It became
clear that some Americans would prefer an authoritarian
state to a democracy where all people receive equal protection, consideration, and benefit.

The rebuilding that followed the Greenwood tragedy was
remarkable and speaks to the agency and resilience of that
wounded community to band together quickly in common
purpose to provide immediate support, for both practical
needs and redress under the law. The community knew how
to tap their own resources and secure help from national
networks of Black civic organizations. African Americans
clearly did not accept the social circumstances that hindered
them, but they were pragmatic in facing and addressing
the situation as it was. And they undoubtedly realized that
starting over somewhere else would not solve the intractable

racial animus, which was widespread, that motivated the White people who had attacked them.

But the outward trappings of revitalization should not gloss over the human toll of such large-scale upheaval. The survivors lived through a warlike attack, with methods perfected abroad and then unleashed on Americans, the likes of which we now know inflict post-traumatic stress disorder and survivor syndrome with adverse effects that can last indefinitely. With their lives at risk—because no one could be sure that the same or worse wouldn't happen again at any time—some stayed, but some decided to leave everything they knew behind for a new beginning elsewhere.

Disruption is a catchword today, but its grotesque implications for life in Tulsa a hundred years ago created scores of internally displaced persons who forged new lives in other parts of the country without the benefit of compassion or aid to get resettled, as still happens across the globe. The repercussions can be felt in the lives of families like my own. Our links to family history were broken as the memories were suppressed by custom, time, and distance, and we lost some of the context that could have helped us make sense of where we were and some of the pain we felt.

In January, after the attempted coup d'état at the Capitol, I published a story in the *Lily* about my family's experience surviving the race massacre. A friend who read my piece told me he cried after realizing it was about Tulsa. His great-grandparents lived through the same event my great-grandmother and grandmother had. They were a solidly middle-class family, but the massacre literally drove them out of Tulsa. They migrated to Detroit, where my friend's grandmother was born, and the family has struggled since. My friend worked hard and is now the epitome of an American success story, but that does not excuse or provide a so-called silver lining to the dark cloud of what his family endured. The hardship that generations of his family carried from the trauma of being hated by their own government and fellow citizens remains a burden.

I lived through the riots of 1960s Oakland, where the community had a reactive relationship with policing; serious, credible allegations of extreme and brutal practices kept tensions high. As I read about the Tulsa events for the first time, I was reminded of those days. The riots were a reaction to systemic abuse and not the abuse itself, as was the case in Tulsa, but I imagined the human reaction was the same: fear and uncertainty. In Tulsa, people's homes were looted and torched. In Oakland, Seventy-Third Avenue needed to be widened so that Athletics and Raiders fans could travel from the I-580 down to the Oakland Coliseum in a straight shot through the heart of East Oakland. Our neighbors' homes were loaded on wide-load flatbed trucks and carted away like children's toys to who knew where. In Tulsa, planes strafed and bombed the neighborhood. In Oakland, helicopters buzzed at night, disrupting our peace. To be clear, there was more than that to life's daily routine in our humble but loving neighborhood, but violent policing and ruthless land development were constants directly from the days of Tulsa—and before. We understood the world we inhabited.

And Mary Jones Parrish understood the world she inhabited. I wondered what I could do with the stories of the lives that were lived, lost, or redeemed in that crucial time—carefully chronicled in my great-grandmother's book—to make more people aware of this tragedy and the ultimate injustice of impunity for the perpetrators. Tulsa's crisis was part of a recognizable pattern that played on repeat in that era, underlining an entrenched commitment to a brutal, dehumanizing system that drove society's abuses of its African American members.

So when the Capitol insurrection unfolded, I recognized what I was seeing. It was the culmination of four years of an administration that had terrified me from its inception for its promise of cruelty. But the worst part was the sense of normalcy that was being thrust on us by leaders who deliberately and determinedly refused to acknowledge the danger of the worst public health crisis in generations and who downplayed the justness of community outrage and protests in the face of the murder of George Floyd in Minneapolis by a uniformed police officer. Instead, these two defining circumstances of 2020 were weaponized in furtherance of a regressive, racist agenda, in the face of which the public was bombarded with messaging that ran counter to objective reality and moral norms. The U.S. president downplayed the lethality of a pandemic, the likes of which had not affected humanity since 1918, when he knew of the widespread disease and death that would result. While the country was reeling from COVID-19, mass public protests in reaction to Floyd's murder were mischaracterized as evidence that the

Black Lives Matter movement was a violent antigovernment movement committed to anarchy.

When a new president was elected and the tide was poised to change from the dangerous direction the country was taking, the world watched a last-ditch effort by a regressive, bigoted cabal and its reactionary mob unfold. Aware of the global context and implications of the events of her time, Mary Jones Parrish had predicted, "If King Mob continues to rule it is only a matter of time until we shall witness some of the scenes of Russia enacted right here on our shores." For her, the national political landscape had international implications. Americans and people abroad expressed a common desire for self-determination, where they could be free to work and live in peace and contribute to society and the world.

As others have been, across time, across geography, across genders, and across peoples, Mary Jones Parrish was a fully realized person, aware of the world and her place in it. She was comfortable in her skin and confident in her abilities. She and women like her were exemplars: vulnerable yet not powerless, empowered yet not superhuman. So why does history have so little to say about her? Why don't more people know about her contribution to interpreting and preserving the history of this pivotal event in American history? Because the powerful shape the historical narrative.

Mary Jones Parrish survived the 1921 Tulsa race massacre, but her legacy almost did not survive erasure. The tragedy would have been all of us being deprived of the voice of the person who told the stories that mattered, the stories of everyday African Americans with normal families, dreams, ambitions, troubles, and lives who were pursuing a normal existence in a great American city. Racist tropes pathologizing Black behavior seek to absolve society's attitudes and actions in distorting the arc of Black life, bending reality with their ability to define what is true. The progress African Americans made in the years after bondage should have been celebrated by our country and compatriots. Instead, progress was punished.

In the current era of historic firsts by African Americans, we must recall that the firsts are not overdue because Black people weren't ready—it is the country that wasn't ready.

>«<

When my daughter was an infant, we were in California staying with my mother, who happened to be dating a White guy at the time. He was driving, and my mother was in the front passenger seat. My daughter, Portia, was in her car seat in the back, happily babbling, as I sat beside her. We were on the I-280, heading down the Peninsula from San Francisco. The Sneath Lane exit came and went, and I casually mentioned that my grandfather died in World War II in Burma and was buried just down the hill in Golden Gate National Cemetery. The boyfriend declared, "That's impossible."

Tsgt. Bruner, who made the ultimate sacrifice for his country, was Florence Parrish Bruner's husband and Mary Jones Parrish's son-in-law. My father was eight years old when he died, and my Uncle Richard was six. The family never recovered.

I continued to gaze out the window, declining to dignify his pronouncement with a reply. I didn't have anything to prove.

Anneliese M. Bruner, the great-granddaughter of Mary E. Jones Parrish, is a writer and editor who has worked in the business, media, and nonprofit sectors. Her writing has appeared in *Honey Magazine, Savoy Magazine, USAID FrontLines*, and *The Lily (Washington Post)*. She was born and raised in San Francisco, with stints in Oakland, and has lived in Washington, D.C., for more than thirty-five years.

Scott Ellsworth is a professor of Afroamerican and African studies at the University of Michigan and the author of *Death in a Promised Land: The Tulsa Race Riot of 1921*, the first comprehensive history of the horrific 1921 Tulsa race massacre. He is helping to lead the ongoing effort to uncover the unmarked graves of massacre victims.

John Hope Franklin (1915–2009) taught at a number of institutions, including Duke University, Howard University, and the University of Chicago. His 1947 landmark study of the African American experience, *From Slavery to Freedom: A History of African Americans*, remains among the most widely read works in the field. He was awarded the Presidential Medal of Freedom in 1995.

Ajamu Kojo is a native of Little Rock, Arkansas, and a graduate of Howard University. He splits his time developing independent film projects, working as a scenic artist on television and film productions, including *Law & Order*, *Boardwalk Empire*, *Vinyl*, and *Bull*, and concentrating on his own artwork. He lives in Brooklyn, New York.

Mary Elizabeth Jones Parrish was born in 1892 in Yazoo City, Mississippi. She moved to Tulsa around 1919 and worked teaching typing and shorthand at a branch of the YMCA. A trained journalist, Parrish gathered eyewitness accounts from survivors of the 1921 Tulsa race massacre and chronicled her own experience fleeing the violence with her young daughter. Those accounts were published in her book *Events of the Tulsa Disaster*, which was privately printed in 1923.